Alexander A. Nelson

Charge of the Lord Chief Justice of England

to the Grand jury at the Central Criminal Court in the case of the Queen against

Nelson and Brand: taken from the shorthand writer's notes, revised and corrected

by the Lord Chief Justice; with occasional no

Alexander A. Nelson

Charge of the Lord Chief Justice of England
to the Grand jury at the Central Criminal Court in the case of the Queen against Nelson and Brand: taken from the shorthand writer's notes, revised and corrected by the Lord Chief Justice; with occasional no

ISBN/EAN: 9783337219314

Printed in Europe, USA, Canada, Australia, Japan

Cover: Foto ©Suzi / pixelio.de

More available books at **www.hansebooks.com**

CHARGE

OF THE

LORD CHIEF JUSTICE OF ENGLAND

TO THE

GRAND JURY

AT THE CENTRAL CRIMINAL COURT,

IN THE CASE OF

THE QUEEN

AGAINST NELSON AND BRAND.

TAKEN FROM THE SHORTHAND WRITER'S NOTES,

REVISED & CORRECTED BY THE LORD CHIEF JUSTICE.

WITH OCCASIONAL NOTES.

EDITED BY

FREDERICK COCKBURN, Esq.,

Of the Crown Office.

LONDON:
WILLIAM RIDGWAY, 169, PICCADILLY.

1867.

At the words "we know not what to do with them," a query should have been appended to the word "not." The word undoubtedly occurs in the deposition of Diana Blackwood, as printed by the Commissioners, but it seems doubtful whether it has not crept in by mistake.

THE interest which has attached to the so-called Jamaica Prosecution, and the great importance of the constitutional and legal questions involved in the recent Charge of the Lord Chief Justice in the case of "The Queen against Nelson and Brand," appear to make it desirable that a fuller and more accurate report of the Charge than could possibly be afforded in the necessarily condensed form of a newspaper report should be placed before the public. The following report has therefore been prepared from the short-hand writer's notes taken at the trial, revised and corrected by the Lord Chief Justice himself. The Chief Justice has also taken this opportunity to add a few notes, either of an explanatory character, or having reference to subjects which, owing to the vast mass of matter with which he had to deal, either escaped his memory at the time, or which from want of time he found it necessary to omit, as also as to one or two matters which have occurred to him since. These notes are distinguished from the references which have been supplied by the editor from the original notes of the Chief Justice, by having the initials of the Chief Justice attached to them. Parts of the Charge have in one or two instances been transposed where the change has appeared to render the meaning plainer, or the reasoning more perspicuous. But the substance of the Charge has been carefully preserved.

CHARGE.

———◆———

IT has been necessary to bring you again into court in consequence of the learned Recorder, upon whom the duty of charging the grand jury of this court ordinarily devolves, being unable, for the reasons which he explained to you on Monday, to take part in any judicial proceeding with reference to the case of "The Queen against Nelson and Brand," which will be brought before you upon an indict-ment for murder. As, therefore, the Recorder is not in a position to afford you that assistance which a grand jury is entitled to expect from judicial authority in a case of difficulty and importance, I have thought it my duty to attend here to-day that I might render you such service as the circumstances of the case require and I am able to afford you. And certainly, whether we look to the principles involved, or to the questions of law which present themselves, this case must be admitted to be one of the greatest difficulty as well as of importance.

Gentlemen, you have heard—for these things have become matter of public notoriety—that this prose-cution is founded upon the fact that a British subject (a Mr. George William Gordon) has been brought to trial before a court-martial, he not being a person in the military service, but a civilian; that by that court-martial, ordered by one of the parties accused, Colonel Nelson, and presided over by the other, Lieutenant Brand, he was condemned for high treason, and sentenced to death, and that sentence having been approved by Colonel Nelson, was executed under it.

The prosecution, as I understand, is founded upon two grounds. In the first place, that there was no jurisdiction in those who tried and sentenced this man to death. In the second, that if there was jurisdiction, that jurisdiction was not honestly, but corruptly, exercised, for the purpose of getting rid of an obnoxious individual.

We will take these two questions in their order; and, with a view first to the question of jurisdiction, I think it important that I should state to you at the outset the facts upon which the question arises. These facts are few, and may be succinctly stated.

It appears that, in the year 1865, a spirit of discontent and disaffection, and of hostility to the authorities, had manifested itself among the negro population in parts of the island of Jamaica. On the 7th of October, in the year 1865, some disturbance took place, on the occasion of a magisterial meeting, at the Court House in Morant Bay, which is, as you are aware, in that island. It is not necessary to go into the circumstances of that disturbance, but it seems to have brought this insurrectionary spirit to a crisis. Immediately after it the negroes in the neighbourhood were evidently in an excited state, and were making preparations for an outbreak; so much so, that on the 10th of October it was thought necessary by the local authorities to communicate with the

Governor, and to apply to him for military assistance.
On the 10th, warrants having been issued against one
or two of the persons who had taken part in the
disturbance on the 7th, upon those warrants being
attempted to be put in execution, forcible resistance
was offered, and on the 11th, the insurgents,
to the number of several hundreds, made their
appearance, more or less in arms. They attacked
the Court House at Morant Bay, in which a
vestry meeting was being held. The volunteers
came to the assistance of the magistrates, but they
were overpowered; the Court House was stormed,
no less than eighteen persons were killed, and upwards of thirty wounded; and from that moment the
negro population in the neighbourhood was in a state
of rebellious insurrection. This spread itself rapidly.
The insurgents attacked the neighbouring estates, destroying property, in two instances taking life, in
others inflicting severe wounds, in others seeking
victims, who, however, managed to escape, and declaring their intention to destroy the male part of the
white population,* and to take possession of all the property in the island. This state of things, as one would
naturally have expected, excited in the minds of the
white population the greatest consternation and alarm.
The military force in the island was but small; the
number of the white population small, very small,
in proportion to that of the black; and the result
was, of course, that terror and alarm pervaded the
whole island. Under these circumstances, the

* They were reported to have declared their intention to reserve the white women for a worse fate; but as to this see note,
p. 157, *post.*

Governor, with the concurrence of a council of war, which he was bound to call, and which he did call, declared the county of Surrey—Morant Bay, where this insurrection broke out, being in the county of Surrey—under martial law, with the exception—and to this I beg to call your particular attention—of the town of Kingston, which is the principal town in that county.

A small military force of 100 men, which had been despatched in consequence of the application made to the Governor on the 10th, was very soon upon the scene of action, and was followed by other troops; and the force so sent, although in point of number comparatively small, was able at once to suppress and crush this outbreak. The moment the soldiers appeared in the field, the whole insurrection collapsed. The negroes everywhere fled, and the only business of the military appears to have been to pursue and take them, and when martial law had been proclaimed, to bring them before the military tribunals. Martial law was proclaimed by the Governor upon the 13th of October. The deceased, Mr. Gordon, resided generally at a short distance from the town of Kingston. He had a place of business at Kingston, and it seems that, for three or four days before his arrest took place under the circumstances I am about to detail to you, he was in the town of Kingston upon a visit to some one there, and was attending to his business as usual. I am not, at this stage of the case, about to enter at all into the merits of the case preferred against Mr. Gordon; the degree in which he was to blame for the dreadful occurrences that took place in Jamaica upon this insurrection, will be matter for consideration by-and-by. It is not necessary to go into that with a view to the question of jurisdiction, which is the one upon which I am now addressing you. It is important that we should keep the various parts of the case distinct and separate, and not mix up matters that have no immediate connection with one another. It is enough here to say Mr. Gordon was generally believed by the authorities and by the white population to have been the instigator of this rebellion, and to be an accomplice with those who were actually engaged in it. It was therefore thought right and necessary to make Mr. Gordon answerable for the offences of which it was believed he had been guilty. The question to-day is, whether the right course was taken to bring him to trial if he had been guilty of crime, or whether his trial and execution were un-authorised, and a violation of the law.

I have told you that Mr. Gordon was staying in the town of Kingston. Martial law had been proclaimed in the county of Surrey, but Kingston had been specially excepted. Warrants having been issued against Mr. Gordon, and that fact having come to his knowledge, it appears that, on the morning of Tuesday, the 17th of October, he proceeded to the house of the General in command of the Forces in Jamaica, General O'Connor, at Kingston, for the purpose of giving him-self up. The Governor, and the Custos of Kingston—the Custos being the title of the principal magistrate in each of the parishes of Jamaica—these two, the Governor and the Custos, came to the General's house, and apprehended Mr. Gordon. They took him on board a war steamer; they conveyed him to

Morant Bay, where he arrived on the evening of the 20th; and, on the day after his arrival, he was put upon his trial before a court-martial, ordered by one of the now accused, Colonel Nelson, who was at that time, with the title of Brigadier-General, in command of the troops which had been sent to Morant Bay for the purpose of suppressing this insurrection. The court-martial was composed of Lieutenant Brand, who is, as you know, one of the accused upon this occasion, and who is a Lieutenant in her Majesty's Navy; of a Lieutenant Errington, also a Lieutenant in her Majesty's Navy; and of a third officer, Ensign Kelly, an officer in her Majesty's 6th West · India Regiment. Before these officers Mr. Gordon was arraigned upon a charge of high treason, and of complicity with those who had broken out in rebellious insurrection against the Government at Morant Bay. Upon this charge he was found guilty and sentenced to be hanged. The sentence was sent for approval and ratification to Colonel Nelson. It was by him approved and ratified, but sent to his superior officer, the General commanding the Forces, General O'Connor, to be by him submitted to the Governor, to see whether the Governor would approve of the sentence, and of its being carried into effect. The Governor did approve of the sentence, and expressed his opinion that it ought to be carried into effect, and, accordingly, on the morning of Monday, the 23rd, Mr. Gordon was hanged; and it is in respect of this execution, and of his having been so put to death, that the present prosecution is instituted.

These being the facts, the first question which presents itself is whether the Governor had authority to proclaim martial law; and, if it should turn out that

he had no such authority, then a further question arises
—namely whether, the parties now accused having
proceeded upon the assumption that the Governor had
authority to proclaim martial law, and that a court-
martial had authority, by virtue of that proclamation,
to try Mr. Gordon and decide upon the charge as it
was submitted to them, and the court-martial having
sentenced him to death, and death having followed
pursuant to such sentence, the putting him to death
under such circumstances amounts or does not amount
to wilful murder.

The first question, therefore, is whether the Governor
had authority to proclaim martial law—a question
obviously of infinite importance, not only in this case,
but in any other similar case which may arise hereafter. Now, one thing is quite clear—namely, that the
power of a Governor to declare martial law can proceed
only from one of two sources. It must either be derived
from the commission which he has received from the
Crown, or from some statute, either of imperial or of
local legislation. It can be derived from no other
source. A Governor, simply as such, would have
no power to declare martial law; but, if the terms of
his commission are large enough to invest him with
such authority as the Crown possesses, and the
Crown has, by virtue of the prerogative inherent in
it, the power to proclaim martial law, the Governor
would have that power. So, again, if, by virtue of
any imperial or local legislation, authority to declare
and exercise martial law has been conferred upon him,
he would be entitled, on the necessity arising, to act
upon that authority. We have, therefore, to inquire,
on the present occasion, whether by virtue of his com-

mission or by virtue of any legislative enactment the Governor of Jamaica was invested with such power.

Before, however, we enter upon the question of whether or not the Governor would have, by virtue of his commission, the power to proclaim martial law and to cause it to be exercised, it is necessary that we should ascertain what is the character of the island of Jamaica as a colony. I do not know if you are aware— possibly not—for these are matters of legal rather than of general knowledge—that from the time of our first colonial acquisitions a distinction has been taken and established by legal authority between two classes of colonies, which are called by the technical names of Crown colonies and Settled colonies. The law with regard to these two classes of colonies is essentially different. A Crown colony, as it is commonly called, is one which has been acquired by conquest, or, what is considered equivalent to conquest, by cession from some other state or power. A settled colony is a colony which is established where land has been taken possession of in the name of the Crown of England, and, being unoccupied, has afterwards been colonised and settled upon by British subjects. With regard to such colonies as are acquired by conquest, except so far as rights may have been secured by any terms of capitulation, the power of the Sovereign is absolute. The conquered are at the mercy of the conqueror. Such possessions keep, it is true, their own laws for the time, because it would be productive of the greatest inconvenience and confusion if a body of people who had been governed by one law, should have that law, with which they are acquainted, suddenly changed for another of which they are totally

ignorant, and of which not only they are totally ignorant, but also the tribunals which are to administer
justice among them. They therefore preserve their
laws and institutions for the time, but subject to this,
that they are under the absolute power of the Sovereign of these realms to alter those laws in any way
that to the Sovereign in Council may seem proper :
in short, they may be dealt with, legislatively and
authoritatively, as the Sovereign may please. Very
different is the case of what is called a "settled"
colony. In such a colony the inhabitants have all
the rights of Englishmen. They take with them, in
the first place, that which no Englishman can by
expatriation put off—namely, allegiance to the Crown,
the duty of obedience to the lawful commands of the
Sovereign, and obedience to the laws which Parliament may think proper to make with reference to
such a colony. But on the other hand they take with
them all the rights and liberties of British subjects—
all the rights and liberties as against the prerogative
of the Crown which they would enjoy in this country.

The law upon this subject, which is one of considerable importance in this case, is thus stated in a
work of high authority, I mean Comyns's Digest :—
"The common law is the inheritance of all the
subjects of the realm ; and therefore in the plantations or elsewhere, where colonies of English are
settled, they are to be governed by the laws of
England. So, if a foreign territory, not inhabited,
be obtained by the Crown of England, all laws of
England bind there."* "In a place occupied by the
King's troops," says Lord Ellenborough, "the subjects
of England would impliedly carry the law of England

* Comyns's Digest—title, "Ley" (C).

with them."* " Your Majesty's subjects carry with them your Majesty's laws wherever they form colonies," said Lord Camden and Lord Hardwicke, in an opinion given by them officially when law officers of the Crown. †

"The common law of England," it was said long ago by an adviser of the Crown, "is the common law of the plantations, and all statutes in the affirmance of the law as passed in England antecedent to the settlement of any colony are in force in that colony, unless there is some private act to the contrary, though no statutes, made since these settlements, are there in force, unless the colonies are particularly mentioned." He adds, in short but emphatic words—"An Englishman, go where he will, carries as much of law and liberty with him as the nature of things will bear."‡ There are other authorities to the same effect. The result of them is shortly and very well stated in Mr. Clark's able work on " Colonial Law." He says this :—" In the case of a colony acquired by occupancy, which is a plantation in the strict and original sense of the word, the law of England then in being is immediately and *ipso facto* in force in the new settlement, and such a colony is not subject to the legislation of the Crown, for the King cannot pretend in that case to the rights of a conqueror; but the subjects of Great Britain, the discoverers, the first inhabitants of the place, carry there with them their own inalienable birthright—the laws of their country."§

* "The King against the Inhabitants of Bampton." 10 East's reports, p. 288.

† 1 " Chalmers' Opinions," 207.

‡ Richard West, afterwards Lord Chancellor of Ireland. 1 " Chalmer's Opinions," p. 206.

§ Clark's "Summary of Colonial Law," p. 7.

Such being the law, we have to inquire to which of the two classes to which I have referred Jamaica belongs. Now, it is quite true that Jamaica was originally acquired by conquest. It was taken by an English force which landed upon the island in the year 1655. It had previously belonged to the Crown of Spain, and was inhabited by a Spanish population, with the negro slaves whom they had introduced for the purpose of cultivating the land. But the colony, once a flourishing one, had fallen into decay, and the population had been reduced to a very limited number. Historians say there were not above 1,500 Spaniards left in the whole island. It appears that on the occasion of the conquest by the English the best portion of the Spanish population at once quitted the island. A few, however, remained, while the negroes withdrew to the mountains, which are in the centre of the island, and are lofty and inaccessible, and were covered—as I believe they are, to a great extent, to this day—with forests, and there established themselves in a state of wild, savage independence, and there, from that time to the present, they have remained, sometimes occasioning great difficulty and trouble to the English Government, but upon the late occasion affording valuable assistance as auxiliaries in suppressing this negro insurrection. They are the people known by the name of Maroons. They have nothing in common with the other negroes except their colour and their African origin.

The Spaniards made an attempt in 1657 to regain possession of the island. They landed in some force, but were repulsed by the English soldiers, and compelled to withdraw; and upon that occasion the rest of the Spanish population, which had not left the island upon the occasion of the first conquest in 1655, took the opportunity of quitting it,* and if one may believe the historians who have written upon the subject of Jamaica, the entire Spanish population disappeared from the island, leaving only the Maroons in the mountains. Therefore, although Jamaica was in this way acquired by conquest in the first instance, yet at the time the English went to settle there it was in fact unoccupied. For, it was after the departure of the Spaniards that the English proceeded to go out and settle in Jamaica. Cromwell, before the end of his reign, made some attempts to get persons to settle in the island, but nothing effectual appears to have been accomplished. When the Restoration took place, Charles the Second and his ministers had the good sense to see that Jamaica would be a most valuable acquisition if they could get it properly peopled. The King used his best endeavours to promote that object. In the first place, he sent out a commission to Colonel D'Oyley, who had been in command of the forces which had previously had possession of the island, and although that officer had been in the service of the Commonwealth, the King thought it wise to continue him in his command, and in the year 1661 sent him out a commission, appointing him to be governor. Grants of land were offered to those who would settle in the island, and at the same time the King issued a proclamation that all children of English subjects who went to settle in Jamaica, though born out of the King's dominions, should have all the rights and liberties of freeborn Englishmen.* Thus encouraged, colonists were soon found to settle in the island. The circumstances of the time were

* Printed at the head of the Jamaica Statutes.

peculiarly favourable to such a result. Many persons who believed themselves obnoxious to the new government, or whose hopes had been disappointed by the restoration of monarchy, were glad to find a refuge or a home in a distant colony, and the King's government was wise enough to throw no obstacles in their way. The spirit of adventure which had burned so fiercely in the previous century had not yet died out, and the prospect of plunder on the commerce and wealth of Spain in the New World attracted many daring spirits to the new colony as a convenient spot from which to carry on their operations. Thus Jamaica was quickly peopled—peopled by Englishmen who settled on lands unoccupied and destitute of other inhabitants.*

Under these circumstances, I can entertain no doubt that Jamaica is entitled to the character of a settled colony. The land was conquered, but the inhabitants by whom it was settled were not. The land was unoccupied when Englishmen went out to settle on it. The settlers who went to inhabit it were not a conquered people, but freeborn Englishmen. They found no Spanish law or Spanish institutions. There was neither a Spanish population who could be treated as vanquished, and therefore at the mercy of the conqueror, nor could there be any Spanish law, or Spanish tribunals to administer it : for which reasons the doctrine of the supremacy of the Crown over a conquered colony, or, rather, over a conquered people— for this is the true foundation of the absolute power of

---

* For fuller details see Edwards' "History of the West Indies," vol. i., book i., chapters 2 and 3; and Mr. Montgomery Martin's interesting and instructive history of the British Colonies, under head of Jamaica.

the Crown—can have no application. But it does not at all rest here. There has been considerable legislation upon the subject. Charles II., in addition to the commission to Colonel D'Oyley, shortly afterwards sent out Lord Windsor to be the governor of the island, with a commission, not only, as had been given to Colonel D'Oyley, to establish a council by popular election, to be the council of the governor, but with authority to call an assembly, to be constituted by popular election, with legislative power in the colony. At first, under that commission, the Assembly had only power to pass laws which were to remain in force for two years. The first Assembly was called in 1664. · Lord Windsor, who did not remain in the island, was succeeded by Sir Thomas Modiford, who called the first Assembly together, and the first Act they passed was that all the laws and statutes of England should be the law of Jamaica. This, I think, was a work of supererogation, for this consequence would have followed from the circumstances in which the colonists were placed without any legislation. But to make the matter sure they passed this Act. Disputes soon afterwards arose between the Assembly of Jamaica and the Government at home upon the subject of the restriction upon their legislative power in respect of the time for which their Acts were to endure, a restriction with which they were much dissatisfied. After a time the King gave way, and in 1680 a new commission was sent out, by which the Assembly were to have power to make laws which should have permanent operation, subject always to such laws being allowed by the King in Council in England. Much about this time hot disputes arose between the Assembly and the Governor upon a subject which has very often given rise to dissensions between rulers and their subjects—namely, the question of taxation. The Governor desired to have a permanent revenue. The Assembly was unwilling to part with the power which the control of the public purse gives, and they refused to do more than vote supplies from time to time. The result was that for sixty years the Assembly of Jamaica was in a constant state of conflict with the Governor and with the Government at home, and always upon this same subject.

The first Act, which provided that the laws of England should be the laws of Jamaica, expired at the end of two years. From time to time the Assembly, after they had the power of permanent legislation, passed similar Acts. But the Government at home disallowed them, possibly from a reluctance to concede absolutely to the colony the right of self-taxation, while the disputes between the Assembly and the Governor continued. However, in the year 1728, upon the accession of George II., a compromise was come to. The legislature of Jamaica agreed to grant certain customs' duties, and other sources of income, as a permanent revenue for the local government of the island, and it was arranged that they should add to the Bill a clause declaring that whatever of the laws and statutes of England had ever been in force in the colony should be considered as the law of Jamaica. This Bill received the royal assent and became law.* Therefore, inasmuch as the Act of 1664, which for the two years that had ensued after its enactment was undoubtedly operative, had established that the laws and statutes of England were during that time in force in the colony of Jamaica, this

* 1 Geo. II. c. i. of Jamaica Statutes.

B

was sufficient to bring the matter within the scope of the enactment of the Statute of 1728; and accordingly it stands fixed by legislative enactment, assented to by the Crown, that the laws of England are the laws of Jamaica. The Act of 1728 has been repealed, and an Act of the 8th of the Queen substituted for it; but the latter statute contains a similar enactment. In point of fact the law of England has ever been the law of Jamaica, except so far as it has been modified by local legislation; and the right of self-taxation—one of the rights incidental to a settled colony, but not to a Crown colony—has never been interfered with or contested.

But there is also judicial authority on the point—the considered and deliberate opinion of the Court of King's Bench, delivered by one of the greatest, if not the greatest, Judge who ever sat in Westminster Hall: I mean Lord Mansfield. In a case of Campbell v. Hall,[*] which was before the Court of King's Bench in 1774, the constitution of Jamaica came incidentally into question. The cause indeed turned upon the constitution of the island of Grenada, in which island—as it had been acquired by conquest from the French—the King in Council had asserted the right of imposing taxes without the assent of the inhabitants, which right it was the object of the action to try. On behalf of the plaintiff, who resisted the tax, the case of Jamaica was referred to as an instance of a colony, in which, though acquired by conquest, the right of the Crown to impose taxes had never been asserted, but the right of self-taxation had from the first been acknowledged. But Lord Mansfield, in giving the judgment of the Court, disposed of this argument by showing that Jamaica was not a

* Reported in Cowper's "Reports," Vol. I., p. 204.

conquered colony. "I have," he said, "on former occasions traced the constitution of Jamaica, as far as there are papers and records in the offices, and cannot find that any Spaniard remained upon the island so late as the Restoration; if any, there were very few. To a question I lately put to a person well informed and acquainted with the country, his answer was, there were no Spanish names among the white inhabitants; there were among the negroes. King Charles II. by proclamation invited settlers there; he made grants of lands; he appointed at first a governor and council only; afterwards he granted a commission to the governor to call an assembly. The constitution of every province immediately under the King has arisen in the same manner; not from grants, but from commissions to call assemblies. And therefore, all the Spaniards having left the island or been driven out, Jamaica from the first settling was an English colony, who, under the authority of the King, planted a vacant island, belonging to him in right of his Crown."

Whether, therefore, we consider the question with reference to principle, to legislation, or to judicial authority, it appears to me impossible to arrive at any other conclusion than that Jamaica is a settled and free colony, the inhabitants of which are entitled to all the rights and liberties to which the subject is entitled at home. I have been the more particular in establishing this position because I have some reason to think that a different view has lately been taken by persons in authority.[*]

---

[*] It follows from what has been said that the question of the power to put martial law in force in Jamaica is not affected by the precedents of Demerara, Ceylon, or any other Crown colony, as in these the power of the Crown is absolute.—A. E. C.

This being so, it follows that the governor, assuming, as I do for the present purpose, that his commission confers on him all the executive power of the Crown in the government of the island, can have no further power to declare martial law, as derived from his commission, than that which the Sovereign would have. We are, therefore, brought face to face with this great constitutional question—Has the Sovereign, by virtue of the prerogative of the Crown, in the event of rebellion, the power of establishing and exercising martial law within the realm of England? So far as this country is concerned, this may be a question of no practical importance. We may look into the long vista of coming years and feel happily satisfied that the question is not likely to arise here. Years of beneficent government have amongst Englishmen changed the abstract duty of loyalty into a sentiment—I had almost said an instinct: the sense of duty has become blended with devotion and attachment to the Sovereign. But this, it is sad to think, is not the case throughout the whole of her Majesty's dominions. We know that only recently, in the sister island, where generations of misrule and of political and religious tyranny and oppression in past times have engendered a spirit of disaffection which even now, when all grievance of every sort and kind—with perhaps one single exception—certainly all political grievance—has been removed—still remains, and of which designing and wicked men take advantage to produce disturbance and insurrection among the inhabitants—we know, I say, that, only recently, her Majesty's Government had under their consideration whether it would be proper to apply martial law.

And though a wise Government would always—
and I doubt not the present Government would
have so done—apply to Parliament for its sanction
to such a proceeding, a case of emergency might
arise when Parliament was not sitting, and when
it could not be called together in sufficient time,
and the Government would therefore find itself placed
in the responsible position either of omitting to have
recourse to means by which insurrection and rebellion might be more effectually suppressed, or, on the
other hand, of authorising the action of martial law,
when, possibly, all proceedings under it for want of
authority would be illegal, and those who took part in
it might be made civilly or criminally responsible in
courts of justice afterwards. The same observation
obviously applies to the governor of a colony. The
question, therefore, is certainly one of the gravest importance. Fortunately, Gentlemen, we have here
nothing to do with the policy of the question : that
is a matter for the legislature alone ; and it may be
that the question is one that ought to receive legislative solution. We, sitting here, have only to
deal with the law, so far as we can ascertain it—
to deal with the law and with nothing else. We
need not trouble ourselves with the consideration of
whether there ought to be such a thing as martial law
or not : the question for us is whether there is such a
thing, and whether the Crown has the power, and
whether the representatives of the Crown in our
colonies abroad have the power, to call it into
action. And if martial law can thus be called into
existence, then arises the all-important question, what
this martial law is. For, of late, doctrines have been

put forward, to my mind of the wildest and most startling character—doctrines which, if true, would establish the position that British subjects, not ordinarily subject to military or martial law, may be brought before tribunals armed with the most arbitrary and despotic power—tribunals which are to create the law which they have to administer, and to determine upon the guilt or innocence of persons brought before them, with a total disregard of all those rules and principles which are of the very essence of justice, and without which there is no security for innocence.

I find such doctrines as these laid down: "Martial law is arbitrary and uncertain in its nature, so much so that the term law cannot be properly applied to it." Again: "When martial law is proclaimed, the law is the will of the ruler, or rather the will of the ruler is law." Again: "When martial law is proclaimed, there is no rule or law by which the officers executing martial law are bound to carry on their proceedings; it is far more extensive than ordinary military law; it overrides all other law; it is entirely arbitrary." Lastly, I find in print this startling proposition: "Martial law is, in short, the suspension of all law but the will of the military commanders intrusted with its execution, to be exercised according to their judgment, the exigencies of the moment, and the usages of the service, with no fixed and settled rules or laws, no definite practice, and not bound even by the rules of military law."* Now, these doctrines having been propounded with some pretence of authority, it is high time they should be brought to the test of judicial determination. At all

* Finlason on Martial Law, p. 107.

events, of this I am sure—that if such is the system of law under which British subjects can be tried for their lives or their liberties, it is time that Parliament should interpose and put some check upon a jurisdiction so purely arbitrary, despotic, and capricious as that which is pointed at in the language to which I have referred. The difficulty one has in dealing with this subject is that, with the exception of the authority of the persons making these assertions, I find no authority at all for any such doctrines. They seem to me, I must say, as unfounded and untenable as, in my judgment, they are mischievous, I had almost said, detestable; and those who propound them appear to me to incur a serious responsibility not only towards those who may be made the victims of so vicious a system, but also towards those who, led on by such assertions, may, by acting on the faith of them, find themselves some day called upon to answer, civilly or criminally, for a violation of the law. It is, therefore, of the utmost importance that these doctrines should be thoroughly sifted, that we may see whether they rest upon any firm or solid foundation of law or authority. And I say that before such doctrines—doctrines so repugnant to the genius of our people, to the spirit of our laws and institutions, to all we have been accustomed to revere and hold sacred—are countenanced and upheld in an English court of justice, we ought to see that there is sufficient authority for the assertion that British subjects can be thus treated. For, it must not be forgotten that whatever may be the charge upon which a man is accused, though he may be a rebel, though he may be the worst traitor that ever was brought to the block, he is still a subject, and entitled, when brought to justice, to those safeguards which are of the essence of Justice, which have been found by experience to be necessary to prevent the rash conclusions and hasty judgments, which even men experienced in the administration of justice are at times liable to form—to prevent, what sometimes happens, innocence from being confounded with guilt, on appearances which a more thorough and patient investigation would have placed in a different light—safeguards more especially required in times of excitement and passion, when the minds of men are more apt to be led astray.

In the first place, then, we have to consider whether there is such a thing as martial law in the sense in which it is used by those who talk of it with reference to the trial of civilians—whether in this sense there is such a thing as martial law known to the law of England. And feeling, as I have done, the vast difficulty, and at the same time the vast importance, of the subject, I have thought it impossible to do justice to it without endeavouring to trace the history of martial law back to its fountain-head, to see when it originated in its application to civilians—and when, and where, and how it has been exercised. I cannot but think that the question is capable of solution in this way only, and that in order to get to the bottom of the subject, it is necessary carefully to trace, in all its phases, the history of the military law of this country. And partly with the desire of satisfying my own mind, partly from a desire of doing my duty towards you, partly also from thinking that in a question of this great national importance it is of the utmost consequence to see what light history can throw upon the subject, I have taken some pains to ascertain the facts connected with it, and I trust I shall not be wearying you, the subject being one of such interest and importance, if I give you the result of such researches as I have been enabled to make.

Let us see when martial law has ever been applied in the history of this country. But on entering upon this investigation we must carefully eliminate from it that which does not properly belong to it. We must bear in mind that we are dealing with cases in which it is admitted that men cannot be put to death or punished . without some form of trial. We are not dealing with the case of rebels killed on the field of battle, or put to death afterwards without any trial at all. A rebel in arms stands in the position of a public enemy, and therefore you may kill him in battle as you might kill a foreign enemy. Being in the position of a public enemy, you may refuse him quarter—you may deal with him in this respect also as with a foreign enemy. And we must not confound with martial law applied to civilians, as we are now dealing with it, what has been commonly done in many epochs of our history in the treatment of rebels taken in the field. Many instances will be found in English history of men being put to death who have been taken in the field, or taken immediately after some decisive battle. You will find instances enough of that sort, but that is not the question with which we are dealing to-day.

So far as I am aware, the first application of anything that can be called martial law took place in the reign of Richard II. There was, indeed, a trial in the reign of Edward II., which historians speak of as a trial by martial law—I mean the trial of the Earl of Lancaster, who had been in rebellion against the King, and who, having been taken, was brought before the King and a certain number of his peers, was tried for high treason, sentenced to death, and executed. Historians, and even legal authorities, have called this a trial by martial law. I very much doubt its having been so, for I have read the whole record of the proceedings, as set out at length in Rymer's "Fœdera,"* and they do not appear to have any reference to martial law at all. The Earl, it seems, was tried by the King and certain of his peers, instead of being tried, as he ought to have been, by his peers in Parliament. It was an irregular trial, undoubtedly, but I question very much whether it was a case of martial law, though, as the trial did not take place before the proper tribunal, it has been treated as such. At all events the attainder was reversed in the subsequent reign, on the ground that the whole proceeding had been irregular, the ordinary courts having been then open, before which the case ought to have been brought. An instance of what has been called martial law occurred in the case of the popular insurrection in the reign of Richard II. When Wat Tyler had been killed, and his followers had been discomfited, it appears that execution was done upon numbers of them, but without any form of trial, or ceremony of any sort. It was, however, thought necessary, even in those days of comparative lawlessness, to have an Act of Indemnity for the executions that had taken place in this irregular manner. An Act was passed, the 5th of Richard II., c. 6, which had this quaint

* Vol. iii., p. 936.

title: "The King's pardon to those who repressed and took revenge of his rebels." The Act recites that "the lords and gentry of the kingdom and others had, in the insurrection of the villeins and malefactors, punished those villeins and traitors without due process of law, and otherwise than according to the laws and usages of the realm;" and the King then proceeds to grant a statutory pardon. Subsequently to this, in the civil wars in the reigns of Henry IV. and Henry VI., a practice sprang up, which was carried to a lamentable excess, of executing as rebels those who were taken in the field. Each of the contending factions, during the wars of the houses of York and Lancaster, as they were alternately successful in battle, executed, without any form of trial whatsoever, the prisoners who fell into their hands. Ordinary persons, when it was thought proper to take vengeance upon such persons, were put to the sword; men of rank and distinction were sent for execution immediately from the field, or perhaps executed within a day or two after, but always without form of trial. The first instance I can discover in which anything under the name or pretence of martial law, in the sense in which we are talking of it—that is, not of law exercised upon persons in rebellion, taken in arms or in hot pursuit from the field, and which, if it can be called law at all, may more properly be called the law of arms or law of the sword than martial law—but of law exercised in the form of trial, is in the reign of Henry VII., and I think it very doubtful what the martial law was that historians speak of there. After the battle of Stoke, in which the King entirely discomfited, with a prodigious slaughter, the faction which sought to place the Pretender, Simnel, on the throne—some days after the victory, when tranquillity and order had been entirely restored, and every vestige of insurrection had disappeared—it occurred to that subtle and avaricious monarch that it might be very convenient to hunt up those who, although they had not taken arms and appeared in the character of rebels in the field, had been aiders and abettors and fomenters of the recent troubles—not so much, indeed, with the desire of taking personal vengeance upon them as of making their offences a source of profit; for to do Henry VII. justice, it was not blood that he was greedy of, but gold. "He made," says Lord Bacon, his historian, "a progress from Lincoln to the Northern parts, though it were indeed rather an itinerary circuit of justice than a progress. For all along as he went, with much severity and strict inquisition, partly by martial law and partly by commission, were punished the adherents and aiders of the late rebels. Not all by death, for the field had drawn much blood, but by fines and ransoms, which spared life and raised treasure."* What Lord Bacon here means by "martial law"—what was the form of the proceeding—what the precise character and nature of it—he does not explain. It was some summary process, no doubt, differing from that of the ordinary tribunals of the country. The result was, I believe, that very few persons were put to death, as everybody who could find the means of buying himself off took care to do so. I dare say if anybody at that time of day had questioned the right of the King to institute such a proceeding, or the propriety of his

* Bacon's Works, vol. v., p. 36.

doing so, he would have found himself in a very awkward situation, and would have had cause to repent of his folly. But, on the other hand, I think it impossible to entertain the shadow of a doubt that these proceedings were utterly illegal. If it be true that you can apply martial law for the purpose of suppressing rebellion, it is equally certain that you cannot bring men to trial for treason under martial law, after a rebellion has been suppressed. It is well established, according to the admission of everybody, even of those who go the farthest in upholding martial law, that the only justification of it is founded on the assumption of an absolute necessity—a necessity paramount to all law, and which, lest the commonwealth should perish, authorises this arbitrary and despotic mode of proceeding; but it never has been said or thought, except perhaps by King Henry VII., that martial law could be resorted to when all the evil of rebellion had passed away, and order and tranquillity had been restored, for the mere purpose of trying and punishing persons whom there was no longer any sufficient cause for withdrawing from the ordinary tribunals and the ordinary laws.

There are, no doubt, some remarkable instances of the application of what is called martial law, but they are instances, not of martial law applied for the purpose of suppressing rebellion, but for the purpose of punishing particular offences or acts which the Government was desirous of preventing; and in every one of them the exercise of martial law was clearly illegal. We have three such instances of martial law in the reign of King Edward VI., upon the occasion of the popular insurrections which took place about that time. You are doubtless aware that that reign was remarkable for the tumultuous state into which the people had got. It was a time when the whole social fabric seemed shaken to its very foundations. The people were everywhere in a state of turbulence and insurrection, it may be said of rebellion, arising in the main from the want and destitution into which the working classes had been brought, and which different causes had concurred in occasioning. In the first place, the monasteries had in the preceding reign been suppressed; and the monasteries, while they existed, had given employment to the labouring class, while to those who were incapable of employment they afforded the means of subsistence— for whatever faults and vices may be ascribed to the monastic institutions, at least we must do them the justice to say that they did their duty towards the poor and destitute classes of the community, and supplied to them that means of subsistence which legislation has since supplied, but which at that time they would otherwise have been entirely without. Those who succeeded to the possessions and vast estates of the monasteries did not consider themselves under any such obligation, and the result was that the poor were entirely deprived of this means of support. Besides this, there began about that period the system of inclosure— which has since been carried for useful purposes to so great an extent—the inclosure of the commons and waste lands, which at that time of day occupied a very considerable portion of the land of this country, and which were productive of great advantage to the poorer people. This inclosure of the commons and wastes by the great men was felt by the people to be a serious hardship and grievance. There was also the circumstance that, about this time, the profit upon the exportation of wool was so great that a practice had begun to be prevalent of converting the arable land of the country into pasture, the result of which was, of course, to deprive the labouring class of so much of the demand for their labour. Then came, also, the importation of the precious metals, by which the value of money was lowered, and the effect of which was felt in the rise of the price of provisions before a corresponding rise had taken place in the wages of labour. All these things working upon the minds of the lower orders, the result was that in various parts of England most formidable insurrections broke out; amongst others the great insurrection in the West, when 10,000 men laid siege to the city of Exeter. In some parts, too, the people were dissatisfied with the change from the more attractive ritual of the Catholic to the more severe and sober forms of worship of the Reformed religion. The people preferred that which spoke more to their imaginations and senses, and manifested their dissatisfaction at the change which had taken place. This feeling was in many places fomented by the priesthood, and a combination of social and political discontent and religious fanaticism was the result. At Exeter the city very nearly succumbed to the siege which these insurgents laid to it; but fortunately, when it was almost overcome by famine, the royal forces appeared, and the rebels were discomfited and routed. Riots and tumults were at the same time going on in various parts of England for the purpose of pulling down inclosures, and committing other acts of plunder and devastation on the property of the wealthy. It appears that one of the things which the rioters had been in the habit of doing was to rouse the villagers by the sound of the church bells, and in the year in which the siege of Exeter had taken place the following proclamation was issued by the King. It is to be found in Strype's "Ecclesiastical Memorials,"* a work of great research and learning. In it the King prohibits any of his subjects that—

"Neither by drum, tabret, pipe, or any other instrument striking or sounding, bell or bells ringing, opening, crying, posting, riding, running, or by any news, rumours, or tales, divulging or spreading, or by any other device or token whatsoever to call together or muster, or attempt to assemble or muster, any number of people; either to pluck down any hedge, pale, fence, wall, or any manner of enclosures, or to hunt, waste, spoil, desolate, or deface any park, chase, warren, house, lodge, pond, waters, or do any other unlawful act which is forbidden; or to redress any thing which should or might be by the King's Majesty's commission reformed, redressed, or amended: and this upon pain of death, presently to be executed by the authority and order of law martial: wherein no delay or deferring of time should be permitted, as in other causes, being indeed of less importance."

This certainly was a very strong proclamation; but the purpose and effect of it was not to establish martial law in the way which is now suggested. The purpose was not to put down an existing rebellion, but to prevent in the future certain offences, which were only misdemeanours at common law, by converting them into capital crimes, and putting a stop to them by the terror of immediate execution; and as these offences could not be thus treated at law, they were made

* Vol. iii., p. 267.

subject to what is termed in the proclamation martial law. No doubt this was a proclamation which the great men of the kingdom, whose property was being destroyed and devastated by these tumultuous bands, were only too glad to see made, and to have put in force if possible, but I have no hesitation in saying that it was entirely illegal, on the ground that offences cannot be created, or the punishments attached by law to existing offences altered, otherwise than by Act of Parliament.

"This year," says Strype, "began the making of the lord-lieutenants of the counties: whose commissions bore date July 24, 3 Ed. VI., as I find it in a clerk of the Crown's book in the Cotton Library: whose office undoubtedly was first instituted upon occasion of these routs and uproars in most of the counties of England. They were called the King's justices in their commissions, as well as lieutenants, which commissions ran, 'To inquire of all treasons, misprisions of treason, insurrections, rebellions, unlawful assemblies and conventicles, unlawful speaking of words, confederacies, conspiracies, false allegations, contempts, falsehoods, negligences, concealments, oppressions, riots, routs, murders, felonies, and other ill deeds whatsoever; and also accessaries of the same: and to appoint certain days and places for the inquiry thereof: and to be the King's lieutenants within the respective counties, for levying of men, and to fight against the King's enemies and rebels, and to execute upon them martial law, and to subdue all invasions, insurrections, &c.' These commissions were renewed yearly."*

* "Ecclesiastical Memorials," vol. iii., p. 278.

Here, again, I have not the least hesitation in saying that this was a power which the Crown was illegally taking to itself in thus altering the law of the land, and affecting to give to the lieutenants of the Crown in counties authority, not merely to try rebels *flagrante seditione*, which is the utmost that can be contended for, but, generally, to withdraw offenders from the cognisance of the ordinary courts of law, and to try them by martial law.

There is, also, a proclamation of the same King of the year 1552. It appears that the tumultuary insurrections which had marked the commencement of this reign were still going on. The statutes which had been passed against vagabonds and sturdy beggars had been found of no avail, and it was thought advisable to try the effect of martial law. Strype says, " Popular disturbances and tumults seemed now to be very frequent among the common people at the present juncture, which occasioned the severe commission which was given out in the month of March to John Earl of Bedford" [and several other great persons whose names are mentioned], " to put in execution all such martial law as shall be thought in their discretion most necessary to be executed. Instructions," he says, " were given to them in nine articles."* Strype states that there was this commission, and from his known accuracy I suppose he must be right. But he does not give his authority, and I have not been able to find the commission in question. It is not to be found in the great work of Rymer, which is supposed to contain almost all the public acts of state and pro-

* "Ecclesiastical Memorials," vol. iv., p. 31.   Ib. 207.

clamations issued by the various sovereigns of England. At all events, according to Mr. Brodie, the late historiographer of Scotland, a very careful and accurate historian, there is no evidence that this commission ever was acted upon.*

There are two instances in the two succeeding reigns in which martial law was applied to a very extraordinary purpose. Queen Mary issued a proclamation in which she declared that the introduction of heretical and seditious works into this country should be punished by martial law, and that any person found to have such books should be reputed and taken for a rebel, and should be executed without delay, according to martial law;† and in this she was followed, in the opposite direction, by her sister and successor, Queen Elizabeth, who, in 1588, issued a proclamation in which she declared that any person introducing bulls from Rome, or any traitorous works from abroad, should be proceeded against and punished by her lieutenants according to martial law, and should suffer such pains and penalties as the latter should think fit, while their goods and chattels should be forfeited.‡

It was clearly beyond the power of the Crown to apply martial law to such purposes. The proclamation of Queen Elizabeth is not, indeed, characterised by the same degree of absurdity as attaches to that of Queen Mary; for one must not forget the circumstances in which Elizabeth was placed at the time her proclamation is stated to have been issued. She had been twice excommunicated by bulls

---

* "Constitutional History," vol. i., p. 157.
† Strype's "Ecclesiastical Memorials," vol. vi., p. 459.
‡ Strype's "Annals," vol. vi., p. 568.

from Rome, and twice the subjects of her realm had been absolved by the Pope from their allegiance; twice they had been called upon from Rome to set her aside as a heretic.* When the King of Spain sent his Armada to the shores of this country, a bull was issued by which the kingdom was made over to him, and the subjects of the Queen were absolved from their allegiance, and taught to look upon her as an accursed being. About the same time a work of a certain Cardinal Allen had been introduced into this country, and widely promulgated, denouncing the Queen as everything that was infamous and wicked, and calling upon the people to rise against her. She had also been in danger of her life through Babington's conspiracy. Under these circumstances one is not surprised to find that, believing that these denunciations from Rome and this absolving of her subjects from their allegiance might be calculated to work upon her people, at least upon that part of the population which still adhered to Catholicism, she fulminated, on her side, against those who were introducing these dangerous instruments and writings into this country, the denunciation of high treason and the punishment of martial law; but we cannot doubt that she was going altogether beyond the powers with which the constitution of England had intrusted her. This proclamation, however, appears merely to have been used *in terrorem;* it was not followed by any commission even verbally authorising the carrying of it into effect.

* To the first of these bulls Lord Bacon ascribes the Northern Rebellion (Works, vol. ii., p. 43), as is also done in the statute 13 Eliz., c. 2.—A. E. C.

And I may make this observation, once for all, upon
the authority of no less a man than Lord Hale, that
at various periods of our history it was the practice
for the sovereign to issue proclamations and commissions as it were *in terrorem populi*—for the purpose
of operating upon the public mind—but which proclamations and commissions were known to be
beyond the powers and prerogative of the Crown,
and were never acted upon because the penalties
could not be inflicted.* So that too much importance ought not to be attached to such proclamations,
looking to the purpose for which they were used,
and to the fact that very often they were not acted
upon at all.†

* See "Considerations Touching the Amendment or Alteration
of Laws," by Lord Chief Justice Hale. Hargraves' Law Tracts,
p. 94—97.

† Proclamations were far more frequent formerly than they
have been in modern times, and it must be admitted that, when
the constitutional boundaries were not as firmly fixed and ascertained as happily they now are, the prerogative of the Crown was
often attempted to be stretched beyond its proper limits by these
declarations of the royal will. The law on the subject is fully discussed and settled by Lord Coke, with his accustomed weight and
learning, in a memorandum under the head of "Proclamations," in
the 12th part of his reports (p. 74). The result of his reasoning
and of the authorities he cites may be briefly stated. Besides such
as are issued in furtherance of the executive power of the Crown,
proclamations which either call upon the subject to fulfil some duty
which he is by law bound to perform, or to abstain from any acts
or conduct already prohibited by law, are perfectly lawful and
right; and it is said that if, after such a proclamation, the law is
nevertheless broken, the disobedience of the royal command, if not
of itself a misdemeanour, is at all events an aggravation of the
offence. On the other hand, wherever a proclamation purports to
be made in the exercise of legislative power—as if the sovereign

A more serious proclamation of martial law occurred in the same reign, in the year 1596. The same causes which had operated upon the lower orders, and had brought them into a state of insurrection, in the reign of King Edward VI., still continued. No provision had as yet been made for the poor, as was afterwards done by the Act of the 43rd of Elizabeth, and great tumults and disorders were taking place in various parts of the country, arising from the destitution of the lower orders. They were what might have been called in modern times "bread riots"—riots engendered by hunger and destitution; not insurrections directed against the Throne or State. Riots of this description had taken place in the immediate neighbourhood of the metropolis; and it happened that, about this time, the apprentices of London, who have on more than one occasion played a prominent part in times of excitement, being, for some reason or other, discontented and turbulent, joined themselves to these bands of rioters, and a great deal of tumult and disorder took place. The City authorities applied to the Queen and her ministers, and requested that martial law might be put in force against the rioters, from whom they apprehended much danger and mischief.

grants a monopoly or privilege against the rights of the rest of the community, or imposes a duty to which the subject is not by law liable, or prohibits under penalties any act which is not an offence at law, or adds fresh penalties to any offence beyond those to which it is already liable, the proclamation is of no effect; for the Crown has no legislative power except such as it exercises in common with the other two branches of the legislature. The King, says Comyns, "cannot by proclamation alter any part of the common law, statutes, or customs of the realm."—(*Digest, title Prerogative*, D. 3.) —A. E. C.

The result was that the Queen issued a commission to Sir Thomas Wilfred authorising him to put martial law in force, which certainly was a very strong proceeding on the part of her Majesty. The commission is to be found in the 16th volume of Rymer. It is in these words :—

"Forasmuch as we understand that of late there have been sundry great unlawful assemblies of a number of base people in riotous sort, both in our City of London and in the suburbs of the same, and in some other parts near to our said City; for the suppression whereof, although there hath been some proceedings in ordinary manner by the mayor of the said City, and sundry offenders have been committed to several prisons, and have also received corporal punishment, by divers orders of our Council in the Star Chamber at Westminster; and for the stay of the like tumults to follow we have also, by our proclamation published the fourth of this month, charged all our justices and other officers having charge for the keeping of peace to have special regard to the inquisition of all that hereafter shall attempt to commit the like offences, and specially for apprehension of all vagrant persons, and them to commit to prison, and punish according to the laws of our realm: yet for that the insolency of many of the kind of desperate offenders is such as they care not for any ordinary punishment by imprisonment and other severe punishment inflicted on them, therefore we find it necessary to have some such notable rebellious and incorrigible persons to be speedily suppressed by execution to death, according to the justice of our martial law; and therefore we have made choice of you, upon special trust of your wisdom, discretion, and other qualities meet for this purpose, to be our Provost-Marshal, giving you authority, and so we command you, upon signification given to you by our Justices of Peace in our City of London, or of any place near to our said City in our Counties of Middlesex, Surrey, Kent, and Essex, of such notable rebellious and incorrigible offenders worthy to be speedily executed by martial law, to attach and take the same persons, and in the presence of the said justices, according to justice of martial law, to execute them upon the gallows or gibbet openly or near to such place where the said rebellious and incorrigible offenders shall be found to have committed the said great offences. And furthermore, we authorise you to repair with a convenient company into all common highways near to our said City where you shall understand that any vagrant persons do haunt, and calling to your assistance some convenient number of our justices and constables abiding about the said places, to apprehend all such vagrant and suspected persons, and them to deliver to the said justices, by them to be committed and examined of the causes of their wandering, and finding them notoriously culpable in the unlawful manner of life, as incorrigible, and so certified to you by the said justices, you shall by our law martial cause to be executed upon the gallows or gibbet some of them that are so found most incorrigible offenders, and some such also of them as have manifestly broken the peace, sithence they have been judged and condemned to death for former offences, and have had our pardon for the same."*

Thus the Queen certainly authorised Sir Thomas Wilfred to execute martial law, not only upon such persons as should be found engaged in rioting, but also upon such as should be found to be leading incorrigibly vagrant lives. This was clearly beyond the power of the Crown. No one could contend that this most extraordinary exercise of assumed power in declaring that persons who were guilty of rioting only, or (what is still more remarkable) of leading vagrant lives, and who could not give a good account of themselves, and who in that respect should be thought to be incorrigible, being, by the ordinary law, liable only to comparatively slight punishment, should, by some summary

* Rymer's "Fœdera," vol. xvi., p. 279.

process of so-called martial law, be condemned and hanged, was within the competency of the Crown. The sovereign having no power of legislation in these realms except as regards persons in the military service of the Crown, there cannot be a doubt that the act of creating new offences or subjecting existing ones to a new law and a new punishment was altogether an unconstitutional proceeding, and beyond any power and prerogative of the Crown. But I am glad to say nobody was put to death under that proclamation. Sir Thomas Wilfred did, indeed, proceed to take up a certain number of the rioters; but wiser counsels prevailed; they were not put to death by martial law; they were brought before the ordinary tribunals of the country, and punished according to the nature of their offences.*

The next instance of the assertion of the power to declare—or rather to authorise the exercise of—martial law that I have been able to find, was in the reign of James I. In the commission given to Lord Compton on his appointment as Lord-Lieutenant or President in Wales, the King, after directing him to muster the militia of the counties in case of necessity —in short, giving him the ordinary powers of Lord-Lieutenant—goes on to say that having collected the necessary forces from time to time as often as need shall require, he is with them—

"To fight all enemies, traytors, and rebells from tyme to tyme, and them to invade, resist, suppresse, subdue, slea, kill, and put to execution of death by all waies and meanes from tyme to tyme by your discretion. And further to doe,

---

* Brodie's "Constitutional History," vol. i., p. 165, and authorities there cited.

execute, and use against the said enemies, traytors, rebells, and such other like offenders, and their adherentes afore-mentioned from tyme to tyme, as necessitie shall require, by your discretion, the lawe called the martiall lawe according to the lawe martiall; and of such offenders apprehended or being brought in subjection to save whom you shall think good to be saved, and to slea, destroie, and put to execution of death such and as many of them as you shall think meete by your good discretion to be put to death.

" And further, our will and pleasure is, and by theise presents wee doe give unto you full power and authoritie that in case any invasion of enemies, insurrection, rebellion, riots, routes, or unlawfull assemblies, or any like offences shall happen to be moved in any place of this our realme out of the limits of this our commission, that then, as often as need shall require, by your good discretion, or as you shall be directed from us by any speciall commandement, you with such power to be levied within the limits of your lieutenancie as you shall think requisite, or as shall be directed from us as is aforesaid, shall repaire to the place where any such invasion, rebellion, unlawfull assembly, or insurrection shall happen to be made, to subdue, represse, and reforme the same, as well by battaile or other kind of force, as otherwise by the laws of the realm and the lawe martiall, according to your discretion."*

So far as the exercise of these extraordinary powers was concerned, this commission remained a dead letter. There was no invasion, no rebellion, no disturbance of any kind; and no occasion, therefore, presented itself for testing the validity of these powers. It is probable that the commission was based very much on the commissions of lieutenancy which were issued by King Edward VI. Assuming for the present that the Sovereign, or the governor of a dependency to whom the executive powers of the Crown are

* Rymer's " Fœdera," vol. xvii., p. 43.

intrusted, has power to proclaim and exercise martial law in case of rebellion, I know of no authority for saying that, by way of anticipation, such power can be committed to the lord-lieutenant of a county in England, where the Crown can exercise its own power and prerogative, and where the executive government has the authority in such matters; nor can it be contended that the Crown can give to a lord-lieutenant of a county the power, after rebels have been "brought into subjection," to execute martial law upon any one to whom he in his discretion shall think it ought to be applied. For these reasons I think it clear that the commissions of lieutenancy of Edward VI. and James I. were both of them illegal.

I now come to the last instance of these attempts to declare martial law in England. It occurred in the reign of Charles I., a reign in which such a thing was not unlikely to occur. This King, at the commencement of his reign, was desirous of embarking in a continental war, for which purpose, of course, he required supplies. His Parliament, however, were not as ardent in respect of war as the King. They were more desirous of seeing a redress of the grievances under which they thought the subject laboured at home; and the result was that they were very sparing in granting supplies, and did not vote them in a manner adequate to the King's requirements. Having tried more than one Parliament in vain, the King had recourse to that illegal mode of obtaining supplies which was known under the name of benevolences or loans, as a means of extorting money from the subject without the intervention of Parliament. As these attempts met with much resistance, the King, in the interval between the second and third Parliament, had recourse to the practice of quartering soldiers on persons who refused to comply with the demand of these benevolences or loans. Of course, what might well have been expected very soon came to pass—namely, the soldiers quartered in this way upon the subjects, knowing that they were quartered upon persons obnoxious to the King, committed great excesses, and the result was that the King found it necessary to deal with these soldiers by military process; and commissions were issued to try soldiers who were guilty of offences or excesses by martial law.

It appears to have been apprehended that similar commissions might be used for the purpose of subjecting to martial law persons who rendered themselves obnoxious by refusing to comply with the attempted exactions. At all events, such an application of martial law was not impossible;* and when the necessities of the King compelled him to summon another Parliament, the first thing which that Parliament did was to vindicate the rights and liberties of the people of England from this unlawful exercise of the prerogative, by the celebrated Petition of Right, in which such commissions are declared to be unlawful, and it is solemnly asserted that the English subject is not to be brought under martial law. I shall have occasion to call your attention more particularly to the terms

* Mr. Forster, in his admirable life of Sir John Eliot, says—"There were proposals actually before the Council at this time to hang men up who refused press money. Coventry, the Lord Keeper, disapproved, or it might have been attempted."—Vol. i., p. 96, n.—A. E. C.

of this Petition by-and-by—suffice it for the present moment to have thus briefly adverted to it. The King did his utmost to evade giving his assent to the Petition in such a way as to bind him; but he was compelled at last to give his sanction to it in the usual form, and that Petition of Right, the supplemental great charter of English liberty, remains to this hour the unquestioned and unquestionable law of the land, and we shall have to look to it presently to see whether there can be such a thing as martial law within the realm of England: certain it is that from that time martial law has never been attempted to be exercised in the realm of England by virtue of the prerogative.* We have had rebellions since, and

* I say "by virtue of the prerogative." An instance certainly occurred during the great Civil War when a partial application of martial law was made by authority of an ordinance passed by the two Houses of Parliament. In 1644, when the Civil War was going on, the Long Parliament determined to establish martial law to a certain extent, and an ordinance was passed whereby a commission was granted to the Earl of Essex, Captain-General of the Parliamentary Forces, together with twenty-nine others of the nobility, gentry, and principal officers, "or any twelve of them," with full power to hear and determine all such causes as belong to military cognisance, according to certain articles therein set forth. ("Parliamentary History," vol. xiii., p. 299.) These articles related mostly to offences of military cognisance, but there are one or two under which civilians might be tried. By the 1st article, for instance, "No person whatever shall go from London and Westminster, or any part of the kingdom under the power of the Parliament, to hold any communication whatever, either personally, by letters, or messages, with the King, Queen, or Lords of the Council abiding with them, without consent of both Houses, or their committee for managing the war, or the Lord General or officer commanding in chief, on pain of death, or other corporal punishment at discretion." By Article 3 "No person whatsoever,

very serious ones. In the first place there was the rebellion of Monmouth in the reign of James II. Martial law might no doubt have been useful in suppressing that rebellion; but it was not proclaimed. It is true that after the rout and discomfiture of Monmouth's army, Lord Faversham, the King's general, put twenty persons to death. Kirk, on his entry into Taunton, executed nineteen more. He and his ruffian followers committed every species of hideous barbarity in the way of death and torture. But all this was done without form of trial, in anticipation, as it were, of the trials and executions which afterwards took place according to the regular forms of law, under the direction of one whose name will ever be execrated in history—I mean Chief Justice Jeffreys. But in all this there was no martial law, at least in the sense in which we are now speaking of it. Again, we had the rebellions of 1715 and 1745, and in neither of these was martial law attempted to be exercised. It is true that after the battle of Culloden horrible barbarities were perpe-

not under the power of the enemy, shall voluntarily relieve any person being in arms against the Parliament, knowing him to be so, with money, victuals, or ammunition, on pain of death, or other corporal punishment at discretion; nor shall voluntarily harbour any such, on pain of such discretionary punishment." By Article 5 "No guardian or officer of any prison shall wilfully suffer any prisoner of war to escape, on pain of death; or negligently, on pain of imprisonment, and further punishment at discretion." Several military officers were tried under this commission. I do not find any instance of a civilian having been brought to trial under it, unless it was Roger l'Estrange, who was tried for coming to Lynn Regis as a spy, and sentenced to death, though he afterwards escaped; but then acting as a spy has always been deemed matter of military cognisance.—A. E. C.

trated—but not by virtue of martial law. The wounded
who were slaughtered in cold blood on the field, the
day after the battle, or who were dragged from the
neighbouring houses where they had taken refuge and
executed, or who were burned in the house in which
they lay helpless, were not put to death under any pretence of martial law. I rejoice to think that in respect of cruelties which never can be forgotten while
English history lasts, and which outraged and indig-
nant humanity never can forgive—I rejoice, I say,
to think that these things were done without even
the pretence of martial law. I rejoice to think that
the name of law, even of martial law, was not profaned
and polluted by being associated with such atrocities
as these.

Gentlemen, I have now gone through the history
of this country so far as relates to martial law.
I believe I have mentioned every instance in which
martial law has ever been proclaimed or been referred
to. But I own that on this point I speak with considerable diffidence; for I cannot claim to have made
history my special study, and my researches in this
particular matter have necessarily been confined to
the intervals of constant and severe judicial labour;
and historians may therefore very likely be aware of
facts which have escaped me; but, so far as I have
been able to discover, no such thing as martial law
has ever been put in force in this country against
civilians, for the purpose of putting down rebellion.
I own, therefore, that I am a little astonished when
I find persons, in authority and out of authority,
talking and writing about martial law in the easy
familiar way in which they do talk about it, as one of

the settled prerogatives of the Crown in this country, and as a thing perfectly ascertained and understood, when, so far as I can find, it never has been resorted to or exercised in England for such a purpose at all. And if there is no such instance to be found, it certainly is a strong reason to doubt the assertion, however positively made, not only that martial law can be resorted to, but that it can be enforced in the arbitrary, despotic, and uncertain form in which they say it is to be exercised.*

* Hume, indeed, writes as follows:—"But martial law went beyond these two Courts"—he had been speaking of the Court of Star Chamber and Court of High Commission—"in a prompt, and arbitrary, and violent method of decision. Whenever there was any insurrection or public disorder, the Crown employed martial law, and it was during that time exercised not only over the soldiers but over the whole people; any one might be punished as an aider and abettor of rebellion whom the provost-marshal or the lieutenant of a county, or their deputies, pleased to suspect." It will scarcely be believed that after making this sweeping assertion, the only instances the historian has to cite are the proclamations of King Edward in 1552, and those of Queen Mary and Queen Elizabeth, which I have already referred to and explained. But the utter untrustworthiness of this elegant writer but most unscrupulous historian, in respect of this and every other branch of the prerogative, when writing with a view to defend the unconstitutional proceedings of Charles I., has been exposed as it deserved by Mr. Brodie in his "Constitutional History" (vol. i., chap. 2). Mr. Hallam, an historian of a very different stamp from Hume, has, however, in his "Constitutional History" (vol. i., chap. 5) the following passages:—"There may be times of pressing danger when the conservation of all demands the sacrifice of the legal rights of a few; there may be circumstances that not only justify, but compel, the temporary abandonment of constitutional forms. It has been usual for all governments, during an actual rebellion, to proclaim martial law, or the suspension of civil jurisdiction. And this anomaly, I must admit, is very far from being less indispensable, at such unhappy seasons, in countries where the ordinary mode of trial is by jury, than where the right of

On the other hand, it is no doubt true that martial law has been put in force in the sister country. I allude to what took place in Ireland at the close

decision resides in the judge. But it is of high importance to watch with extreme jealousy the disposition, towards which most governments are prone, to introduce too soon, to extend too far, to retain too long, so perilous a remedy. In the fourteenth and fifteenth centuries the court of the constable and marshal, whose jurisdiction was considered as of a military nature, and whose proceedings were not according to the course of the common law, sometimes tried offenders by what was called martial law, but only, I believe, either during, or not long after, a serious rebellion. This tribunal fell into disuse under the Tudors." I cannot help thinking that this eminent historian has here, for once, fallen into error. In the first place, for the assertion of the general use of martial law in this country he has not any instance to adduce beyond those referred to by Hume, and which certainly are insufficient to sustain so large an assertion. But the statement that the court of the constable and marshal ever tried offenders (other than soldiers) under martial law in this country is equally open to exception. Mr. Hallam mentions no instance in which an ordinary subject ever was tried in the marshal's court for any offence committed in this country. Nor could civilians have been tried before that court consistently with the statutes of 8 Richard II., c. 5, and 13 Richard II., c. 2, which expressly exclude from its jurisdiction all cases that could be tried at common law. The office and authority of the High Constable and Earl Marshal (which are dealt with further on) have been amply discussed in the works not only of legal writers, but also of professed antiquaries. In Hearn's "Discourses of Eminent Antiquaries" there are several discourses on the subject. But I nowhere find it stated that the court of these officers ever tried civilians under martial law. Indeed, it appears that in the instances of the irregular application of martial law already referred to, commissions were issued to try offenders where martial law was intended to be enforced. Mr. Brodie considers the fact of no commission having issued after a proclamation of martial law as cogent evidence that the proclamation was not intended to be enforced.—A. E. C.

of the last century; and it may not be unimportant
to turn to that page of history, as calculated to
throw light on the present inquiry. From the
year 1790 or thereabouts Ireland was in a very
agitated state. As early as the year 1795, insurrections of a serious nature were occurring in various
parts of the country; and it would seem that magistrates and persons in authority took upon themselves
to execute a species of martial law without any
authority whatever. But they were the dominant
party; they had a large majority in the Parliament
of Ireland; and it was thought expedient, in order
to prevent open rebellion and all the serious consequences that it entails, to have recourse to means
beyond the ordinary law; but they thought it equally
necessary to obtain Acts of Indemnity. An Act of Indemnity was passed as early as 1796 (36 George III.,
c. 6, of the Irish Statutes) for excesses beyond the
law committed in the year 1795. The Act recites
that—

"During the year 1795 several parts of this kingdom
(Ireland) were disturbed by treasonable insurrection of
persons assuming the name of defenders, and the lives and
properties of many peaceable and faithful subjects were
destroyed, and several of his Majesty's Justices of the Peace
and other officers and persons, in order to preserve the public
peace, the lives and property of his Majesty's faithful subjects,
and to suppress and put an end to such insurrection, have
apprehended several criminals and persons suspected of aiding
and assisting in the said insurrection, and of promoting riot
and tumult, and of harbouring evil designs against his
Majesty's Government, and without due authority have sent
other criminal or suspected persons out of the kingdom for
his Majesty's service, and also used arms, and entered into
the houses and possessions of several persons, and done divers

other acts not justifiable by law, but which were yet so much for the public service, and so necessary for the suppression of such insurrection and for the preservation of the public peace, that the persons by whom they were transacted ought to be indemnified."

This language shows that, even before martial law had been proclaimed, proceedings took place which were beyond the law, and for which an Act of Indemnity was required. An Act in similar terms was from this time passed periodically, I think every six months, by the Irish legislature, till we arrive at the year 1798. In the May of that year, things had assumed so serious an aspect that Lord Camden, the then Lord-Lieutenant, thought it right to issue a proclamation declaring martial law. Martial law was put in force, and many persons were executed under it. In the November of that year a case presented itself, upon which, if an unhappy catastrophe had not brought it to a premature close, we might have had a judicial decision which would have been a guide to us on the present occasion; but it unfortunately failed. Among the most conspicuous of the promoters of the rebellion was a man of the name of Wolfe Tone. He had been to France for the purpose of obtaining the assistance of the French Government of that day to invade Ireland. The French sent a force with ships of war; but the French ships were intercepted by an English fleet, and so the invasion was frustrated. Some of the French ships were captured, and in one of them Wolfe Tone, who was on board of her, was taken. There was no doubt whatever of the active part he had taken in exciting and promoting the rebellion, and as soon as he was landed in Ireland he was brought to trial before a court-martial. He did not at all deny his share in the rebellion that had taken place. He was sentenced to death—to be hanged; but he prayed that, as he was a soldier (for he held military rank in the army of the French Directory), the form of death might be changed, and that he might die the death of a soldier and be shot. This was refused, and he was to be hanged. At the instance of his father, an application was made on his behalf to the Court of King's Bench in Dublin for a *habeas corpus*, on the ground that he had been sentenced to death by a court-martial, and that the martial law was illegal, as the King's courts were sitting, and consequently the ordinary jurisdiction was not superseded. The Court at once granted a *habeas corpus* to bring Mr. Wolfe Tone before them, and upon its being suggested that he had been sentenced to immediate death, and that it was probable that, unless vigorous measures were taken, the sentence would be executed before he could be wrested from the hands of the military authorities, in whose power he was, the Court of King's Bench immediately commanded the Sheriff to proceed at once to the place where Wolfe Tone was in military custody, and to inform the military authorities that a writ of *habeas corpus* was preparing, and to see that Tone was not executed. The Sheriff returned, and stated that the provost-marshal had said he must obey Major Sandys (the commanding officer at the barracks), and that Major Sandys had said he must obey the Lord-Lieutenant. Whereupon the Court ordered the Sheriff to return, and take not only Mr. Tone into his custody, but the provost-marshal and Major Sandys also. The

Sheriff went, but he found Tone dying. Unable to bear the ignominy of an execution by the hands of the hangman, he had cut his throat in prison, and was soon afterwards a corpse, and consequently the question was not solved.* But after this it was thought desirable to supersede the proclamation of the Lord-Lieutenant appointing martial law, and to have statutory authority for its exercise, so as to preclude the intervention of a court of law.

Now, nobody can deny for a moment the power of Parliament to enact that martial law shall be put in force; and, in case of need, a wise government would probably, if it had the opportunity, have recourse to Parliamentary authority for the purpose; the more so as, then, such restrictions and conditions can be placed on the exercise of this anomalous jurisdiction as may insure the observance of those things which are essential to justice, and which tend to secure it from those disturbing influences which in times of public commotion are too apt to operate on the minds of those who may be called on to administer this rude and hasty justice, and to lead them to arbitrary and rash decisions. But here, again, in addition to the Act giving power to establish martial law,† it was thought necessary to obtain an Act of Indemnity in respect of all that had been done under the proclamation of martial law; and accordingly an Indemnity Act‡ was passed by the Irish Parliament, and came into operation on the same day as the other statute. After reciting

---

* A full report of the proceedings in Tone's case is to be found in the 27th vol. of the " State Trials," p. 613.

† 39 Geo III., c. 11.   ‡ 39 Geo. III., c. 3.

that "officers and justices of the peace and others, in order to preserve the public peace and to suppress the insurrections and rebellion, had apprehended several criminals suspected of being concerned therein, and without due authority had sent other criminals or suspected persons out of the kingdom, and had been obliged to punish several of the said offenders even with death, and to do other acts not justifiable by law," the Act gave protection to all who had carried martial law into execution under the proclamation of the Lord-Lieutenant. The Union having taken place, an Act of the United Kingdom* was passed for continuing the power to exercise martial law in Ireland. That statute authorises—

" The Lord-Lieutenant or other chief governor or governors of Ireland, from time to time, during the continuance of the said rebellion, whether the ordinary courts of justice shall or shall not at such time be open, to punish all persons acting, aiding, or in any manner assisting in the said Rebellion, or maliciously attacking or injuring the persons or properties of his Majesty's loyal subjects, in furtherance of the same, according to martial law, either by death or otherwise, as to them shall seem expedient for the punishment and suppression of all rebels in their several districts; and to arrest and detain in custody all persons engaged in such rebellion, or suspected thereof; and to cause all persons so arrested and detained in custody to be brought to trial in a summary way by courts-martial, to be assembled under such authority as the said Lord-Lieutenant or other chief governor or governors shall from time to time direct, and to consist of commissioned officers of the line, fencible or militia regiments, or yeomanry corps, not less in number than seven, nor more than thirteen, for all offences committed in furtherance of the said insurrection and rebellion, whether such persons shall have been

* 43 Geo. III., c. 117.

taken in open arms against his Majesty, or shall have been otherwise concerned in the said rebellion, or in aiding or any manner assisting the same, and to execute the sentences of all such courts-martial, whether of death or otherwise, and do all other acts necessary for such several purposes, provided that no sentence of death shall be given against any offender by such court-martial unless the judgment shall pass by the concurrence of two-thirds at least of the officers present."

It then proceeds to indemnify all who shall act under it from any consequences, criminal or civil. It prevents their acts from being brought within the jurisdiction of the ordinary tribunals at all.

There remains one other statute, and it is an important one. In the year 1833, Ireland being then in a very disturbed state, an Act* was passed "for the more effectual suppression of local disturbances and dangerous associations" in that country. By this Act power was given to the Lord-Lieutenant to proclaim any county or district to be in such a state of disturbance and insubordination as to require the application of the Act; and the 13th section, after reciting that the ordinary tribunals may, in certain cases, in proclaimed districts, be inadequate to the prompt and effectual punishment of the offences hereinafter mentioned, proceeds to enact that the Lord-Lieutenant, or other chief governor or governors of Ireland, and any general or other officer commanding the district, being by him or them duly authorised, may, if he or they shall so think fit, from time to time commission any officers or officer of his Majesty's regular forces, not being under the degree of a field-officer, to convene, assemble, and hold courts-martial within any districts or district so proclaimed, for the

* 3 and 4 Wm. IV., c. 4.

trial of such persons charged with offences committed within such district as any such court-martial shall be directed by warrant or order of the Lord-Lieutenant or chief governor or governors of Ireland, or other officer duly authorised by him or them as aforesaid, to try. The Act then goes on, in section 14, to provide for the constitution of the courts-martial, which are to consist of officers of his Majesty's regular forces, not less than five nor exceeding nine in number. Their proceedings are to be conducted according to the manner of proceeding used by courts-martial holden under the Mutiny Act. No officer is to serve on any such court-martial who shall not have attained the rank of captain in his Majesty's army, or who shall within one month of the time of holding such court-martial be, or have been, in the performance of regimental duty within such proclaimed district. No officer below the rank of a field-officer is to be the president of such court-martial. On trials before such courts the parties, their counsel, and attorneys are to be at liberty to examine and cross-examine the witnesses, and to take notes of the proceedings for the purposes of such trials, as in courts of law; and all prosecutions before such courts-martial are to be conducted by a person or persons thereunto duly authorised by the Lord-Lieutenant. It is furthermore provided, by section 15, that, when the court-martial shall consist of nine members, the concurrence of seven, if it shall consist of less than nine, then the concurrence of at least five members, shall be required. Lastly, by section 16, it is enacted that a serjeant-at-law or barrister of not less than five years' standing shall be appointed by the Lord-Lieutenant to act as Judge-Advocate on every such court-martial.*

These instances of the application of martial law were therefore either under statutory powers, with which no man has, judicially speaking, a right to quarrel, or, when exercised by virtue of the prerogative of the Crown, were followed by Acts of Indemnity; which, to say the least of it, sufficiently implies a doubt of the legality of the exercise of the power.

Gentlemen, I have thrown what light I could from historical sources on this part of the case. Let us next see what can be found in the way of authority, either in the writings of great lawyers, or in judicial decisions, or in the way of statutory recognition or disaffirmance of the prerogative. Now, certainly, as regards the works of legal writers or judicial decisions, not only is there no authority in support of the power to declare martial law, but what authority there is we shall find to be directly the other way. Lord Chief Justice Hale, in his "History of the Common Law,"† speaking of martial law, says that it is "something indulged, rather than allowed, as a law: the necessity of government, order, and discipline in an army being that which alone can give those laws a countenance : *quod enim necessitas cogit, defendit.*" "Secondly," he says, "this indulged law was only to extend to members of the army or to those of the opposite army, and never was so much indulged as

* The power to inflict whipping as a punishment is expressly taken away by this Act.

† "History of the Common Law," p. 35.

intended to be executed or exercised upon others; for *others who were not listed under the army had no colour or reason to be bound by military constitutions, applicable only to the army, whereof they were not parts; but they were to be ordered and governed according to the laws to which they were subject, though it were a time of war.**

* It is plain that, according both to Lord Coke and Lord Hale, even soldiers and sailors could not, at least so far as life was concerned, be tried by martial law in time of peace. "If," says Lord Coke, "a lieutenant or other that hath commission of martial authority in time of peace hang or otherwise execute any man by colour of martial law, this is murder; for this is against Magna Charta, cap. 29, and is done with such power and strength that the party cannot defend himself; and here the law implieth malice."— (*Coke*, 3 *Inst.*, *p.* 52.) "If persons," says Lord Hale, "be listed under a general or lieutenant of the King's appointment under the Great Seal, and modelled into the form and discipline of an army, either in garrison or without, yet as long as it is *tempus pacis* in this kingdom they cannot be proceeded against as to loss of life by martial law; and the same for mariners that are within the body of the kingdom; but their misdemeanours, at least if capital, are to be punished according to the settled laws of the kingdom (3 Car. I., cap. 1, the Petition of Right). Yea, and it seems as to mariners and soldiers at sea, when in actual service in the King's ships, they ought not to be put to death by martial law, unless it be actually in time of hostility; and this appears by the statute of 28 H. 8, that settled a commission to proceed criminally in cases of treason and felony, and by the late act of 13 Car. 2, cap. 9, settling special orders under pain of death by Act of Parliament. But, indeed, for crimes committed on the high sea, the admiral had at common law a jurisdiction even unto death, *secundum leges maritimas;* but this was a different thing from martial law. And this appears also by the statute of 13 R. 2, cap. 2. The constable and marshal, who are the *judices ordinarii* in cases belonging to the martial law, are yet thereby declared to have no jurisdiction within the realm, but of things that touch war, which cannot be discussed nor determined by the common law. It must therefore be a time of war that must give exercise to their jurisdictions, at least in cases of life."—(*Hale*,

Besides this positive statement of Lord Hale, the negative evidence, if I may so call it, which arises from the silence of such great legal authorities as Lord Coke and Sir William Blackstone, in their works on the law of England, is to my mind almost as cogent as their express authority would have been, against this alleged power of declaring martial law and superseding the ordinary tribunals. It is hardly conceivable that such authors as these, when writing on the laws of England, and carefully enumerating every species of law obtaining within the kingdom, would, when they came to speak of martial law, have been wholly silent as to the power of applying it to the trial and punishment of civilians in times of civil disturbance and insurrection, if any power of so applying it had in their opinion existed. Coke's opinion to the contrary was indeed very plainly expressed in the great debate in the committee of the whole House on the Petition of Right. "A rebel," said he, "may be slain in the rebellion; but if he be taken, he cannot be put to death by the martial law."[*] And Rolle, afterwards Lord Chief Justice, and a most learned lawyer, on the same occasion said, "If a subject be taken in rebellion, and be not slain at the time of his rebellion, he is to be tried after by the common law."[†]

I will next call your attention to the opinion of a distinguished judge in the case of Grant *versus* Gould,

Pleas of the Crown, *p.* 500.) Blackstone is evidently of the same opinion, as appears from the passage hereinafter cited from the 1st Commentaries, p. 413. And the recital at the commencement of each successive Mutiny Act is a Parliamentary recognition of the same thing.—A. E. C.

[*] 3 "Rushworth's Collection," vol. iii., App., p. 81.

[†] Ib., p. 79.

which occurred in the year 1792.* Grant was a recruiting-sergeant—that is to say, he was not in fact
in the service at all, but he had been allowed to assume the character of a sergeant in the army, for the
purpose of getting recruits, and he was in the pay
of the Government as a recruiting-sergeant. He
induced two soldiers of the Guards to desert for the
purpose of enlisting in the East India Company's
service, for which he was also enlisting recruits. He
was brought before a court-martial, of which Sir
Charles Gould was president, and was sentenced to
receive a thousand lashes. An application was made
to the Court of Common Pleas for a prohibition to
stop the execution of the sentence, on the ground
that he was not, in point of fact, in the army.
The court, however, adverting to the Mutiny Act
and the Articles of War, by which it is provided that
everybody receiving pay as a soldier shall be considered amenable to the Articles of War, held that they
had no jurisdiction to interfere in the matter, as it
was one of military jurisdiction, and had therefore
been properly brought before a court-martial. Upon
that occasion Lord Loughborough, then Lord Chief
Justice of the Court of Common Pleas, and who
afterwards became, under the title of Lord Rosslyn,
Lord Chancellor of England, makes these observations
on the subject of martial law, that question having
incidentally arisen :—

" Martial law, such as it is described by Hale, and such also
as it is marked by Mr. Justice Blackstone, does not exist in
England at all. Where martial law is established and
prevails in any country, it is of a totally different nature from

* 2 Hen. Blackstone's " Reports," p. 69.

that which is inaccurately called martial law merely because the decision is by a court-martial, but which bears no affinity to that which was formerly attempted to be exercised in this kingdom; which was contrary to the constitution, and which has been for a century totally exploded. Where martial law prevails, the authority under which it is exercised claims a jurisdiction over all military persons in all circumstances. Even their debts are subject to inquiry by a military authority; every species of offence, committed by any person who appertains to the army, is tried, not by a civil judicature, but by the judicature of the regiment or corps to which he belongs. It extends also to a great variety of cases, not relating to the discipline of the army, in those states which subsist by military power. Plots against the sovereign, intelligence to the enemy, and the like, are all considered as cases within the cognizance of military authority.

"In the reign of King William there was a conspiracy against his person in Holland, and the persons guilty of that conspiracy were tried by a council of officers. There was also a conspiracy against him in England, but the conspirators were tried by the common law. And, within a very recent period, the incendiaries who attempted to set fire to the docks at Portsmouth were tried by the common law. In this country all the delinquencies of soldiers are not triable, as in most other countries in Europe, by martial law; but where they are ordinary offences against the civil peace, they are tried by the common law courts. Therefore it is totally inaccurate to state martial law as having any place whatever within the realm of Great Britain. But there is, by the providence and wisdom of the legislature, an army established in this country, of which it is necessary to keep up the establishment.

"The army being established by the authority of the legislature, it is an indispensable requisite of that establishment that there should be order and discipline kept up in it, and that the persons who compose the army, for all offences in their military capacity, should be subject to a trial by their officers. That has induced the absolute necessity of a Mutiny

Act accompanying the army. It has happened, indeed, at different periods of the government, that there has been a strong opposition to the establishment of the army. But the army being established and voted, that led to the establishment of a Mutiny Act."

It is plain, therefore, that in the opinion of this eminent judge there was no such thing within the realm of England as that which is now called "martial law." Lastly, Lord Chief Baron Comyns says—"Martial law cannot be used in England without authority of Parliament "*

So much for authority on this subject.† Let us now

* Comyns's Digest, title "Parliament," H. 23.

† I am indebted to the learning and research of Mr. Spencer Perceval, of the Equity bar, for a reference to an important paper on the subject of martial law, written by the late Mr. Hargrave, with the existence of which I was not acquainted at the time this charge was delivered. It is published in Hargrave's " Jurisconsult Exercitations," vol. i., p. 399. Mr. Hargrave had been called upon to advise, as counsel, as to the means of obtaining the reversal of the attainder of a Mr. Grogan, a gentleman of fortune in the county of Wexford, who, after the proclamation of martial law in Ireland by the Lord-Lieutenant, in 1798, was tried before a court-martial for high treason, condemned, and executed, an act of attainder being afterwards passed against him by the Irish Parliament. Referring to the opinion he had given on that case, Mr. Hargrave writes as follows:—"The question which forced itself in a great degree upon the author's mind, when he was called upon professionally to write an opinion in answer to those who consulted him for the purpose of seeking a repeal of the Grogan attainder, was—whether, independently of the express warrant of an Act of Parliament, and on the mere ground of prerogative power, authority could be given against persons taken into custody for high treason during the heat of rebellion, to try them by martial law for their offence, and to punish them, either by death or in any other way, at the discretion of the court-martial so trying them. Looking to that question, he could not forbear avowing how his

see what we can find in our statutory law. I mentioned to you, in the historical sketch which I troubled you with, that the commission of martial law issued by

mind was affected. But he so avowed himself under a conviction that martial law to such an extent was not the law of England without an express Act of Parliament. He saw the right of putting rebels to death in battle, while the battle lasted. He also saw the right to arrest those found in actual rebellion or duly charged with being traitors, and to have them imprisoned for trial and punishment according to the law of treason. But he could not see that punishing and trying rebels according to martial law was, when Mr. Grogan was tried and put to death, part of the English law as it was administered in England, or even as it was administered in Ireland. On the contrary, he saw such a prerogative doctrine to be inconsonant with several recitals and one enactment in that grand Act of Parliament, the Petition of Right, in 3rd of Charles I. He saw it also to be irreconcilable with the opinions declared, by some of the greatest lawyers of that time, to a committee of the whole House of Commons sitting on martial law, namely, Sir Edward Coke, Mr. Noy, afterwards Attorney-General, Mr. Rolle, afterwards Sergeant-at-law, and author of the abridgment, Mr. Banks, afterwards successively Attorney-General and Lord Chief Justice of the Common Pleas, and Mr. Mason, distinguished both as a lawyer and a member of Parliament; for which opinions the author begs leave to refer to the preservation of them in the appendix to Rushworth's third volume. Further, the author found such a latitude of martial law equally crossed by the doctrines of Lord Chief Justice Hale, as expressed in his manuscript and unprinted collections on the prerogative. This, the author trusts, will, without for the present looking further, sufficiently at least apologise for the strong terms used in those parts of his opinion in the Grogan case, which relate to martial law; even though volumes of cruel and irregular practice during the sad extremities of civil war should be laboriously collected, to overcome the potency of the Petition of Right and of the high, grave, legal authorities the author inclusively relies upon as speaking the same language." The acknowledged reputation of Mr. Hargrave for great learning and profound knowledge of law makes his opinion on this subject one of great authority.—A. E. C.

Charles I. had led to the Petition of Right. Let me now direct your attention more particularly to the terms of that memorable statute—which there is good reason to believe was drawn up by Lord Coke himself—at least to that part of it which is applicable to the present question.

After dealing with several other grievances arising from the unlawful exercise of the prerogative, the petition proceeds as follows:—

" Whereas of late great companies of soldiers and mariners have been dispersed into divers counties of the realm; and the inhabitants, against their wills, have been compelled to receive them into their houses and there to suffer them to sojourn, against the laws and customs of this realm, and to the great grievance and vexation of the people.

" And whereas, by authority of Parliament in the 25th year of Edward III., it is enacted that no man shall be forejudged of life or limb against the form of the Great Charter and the laws of the land; and by the said Great Charter and other laws of this realm no man ought to be adjudged to death but by the laws established in this realm; nevertheless divers commissions under the Great Seal have been issued forth, by which certain persons have been appointed commissioners, with power and authority to proceed within the land according to the justice of martial law against such soldiers or mariners, or other dissolute persons going with them, as should commit any murder, robbery, felony, mutiny, &c., and by such summary course and order as is agreeable to martial law, and as is used in armies in time of war, to proceed to the trial and condemnation of such offenders, and them cause to be executed and put to death according to martial law. By pretext whereof some of your Majesty's subjects have been by some of the said commissioners put to death, when and where, if by the laws and statutes of the land they had deserved death, by the same laws and statutes also they might, and by no other ought, to have been judged and executed. And also sundry grievous offenders, by colour thereof claiming an exemption, have escaped the punishments due to them by the laws and statutes of this realm, by reason that divers officers and ministers of justice have unjustly refused or have forborne to proceed against such offenders according to the same laws and statutes, upon pretence that the said offenders were punishable only by martial law, and by authority of such commissions as aforesaid; which commissions are wholly and directly contrary to the laws and statutes of this realm.

" They do therefore humbly pray that your Majesty would be pleased to remove the said soldiers and mariners, and that your people may not be burdened in time to come; and that the aforesaid commissions for proceeding by martial law may be revoked and annulled, and that hereafter no commissions of the like nature may issue forth to any person whatsoever to be executed as aforesaid, lest by colour of them any of your Majesty's subjects be destroyed or put to death contrary to the laws and franchise of the land."

I have lately seen in print (I confess to my great astonishment) that the Petition of Right is of no efficacy beyond the shores of this country, and that it can have no application to the case of martial law proclaimed by a Governor of Jamaica. This must have proceeded from an entire misconception of the character and effect of this statute. It is not an enacting statute at all. It is not a statute by which any new limitation was put upon the prerogative of the Crown, or by which the subject acquired any new rights or immunities against the prerogative. It is a statute declaring where, according to the law and constitution of this country, the prerogative of the Crown ends and the rights and liberties of the subject begin. Therefore, if the common law of this

E

country is, as I have already shown it to be, applicable to Jamaica, it follows that if the Petition of Right would prevent the exercise of martial law by virtue of the prerogative in England, it must of necessity do so in Jamaica. Whether it does or does not put a restraint on this exercise of the prerogative is another matter: what I am now pointing out is, that if the Petition of Right establishes that the application of martial law to the subject in the time of rebellion in England is unlawful, it beyond question equally does so with reference to martial law in the island of Jamaica.

Two views have been propounded of this celebrated statute. The one that its effect is limited to commissions such as those of which the Commons had more immediate cause to complain, and especially to commissions issued in time of peace; the other that it was intended to prevent the exercise of martial law against the subject, under any circumstances, and even as against the soldier, except in the case of "armies in time of war." The latter would appear to have been the view of Lord Hale, and the words of the statute are certainly large enough to embrace the more general position; nor is it at all probable that the Commons, many of whom must have foreseen that, as things were then going on, armed resistance to the encroachments of the prerogative might become inevitable, intended to leave the subject, in the event of popular commotion, at the mercy of martial law.

We have next to consider the effect of the recitals in the Mutiny Acts. Standing armies in time of peace were in the earlier ages of our history unknown. The practice of maintaining such an army in time of peace was first introduced by King Charles II., but to the limited extent of 5,000 men. James II., however, raised the number of his forces to 30,000 men; and if his army had been willing to support him in his designs on the liberties of the country, those liberties would have been in imminent peril. When, therefore, William of Orange was invited to take the throne of these realms, the Declaration of Rights, and afterwards the Bill of Rights, laid down the constitutional maxim that "the maintenance of a standing army in time of peace without the consent of Parliament was contrary to law." Nevertheless, as the exigency of the times required, as they still require, a standing army, Parliament, from that time to the present, gives annually its consent to the maintenance of such an army. The preamble of the first Mutiny Act (1st William and Mary, Session 2, cap. iv.) is in these words :—

"Whereas the raising or keeping a standing army within this kingdome in time of peace, unlesse it be with the consent of Parlyament, is against law; and whereas it is judged necessary, by their Majestyes and this present Parlyament, that during the time of warr severall of the forces which are now on foote should be continued, and others raised, for the safety of the kingdome, for the common defence of the Protestant religion, and for the reducing of Ireland; and whereas no man can be prejudged of life or limb, or subjected to any kinde of punishment by martiall law, or in any other manner than by the judgment of his peeres, and according to the knowne and established laws of this realme; yet, nevertheless, it being requisite for retaining such forces as are or shall be raised during this exigence of affaires in their duty, that an exact discipline be observed; and that soldiers who shall mutiny or stirr up sedition, or who shall desert their

Majestyes' service, be brought to more exemplary and speedy punishment than the usual forms of law will allow :"

After which the Act provides for the assembling and constitution of courts-martial, for the oath of members, for the punishment of desertion, mutiny, sedition, false musters, &c., and is ordered to be read at the head of every regiment, troop, or company, at every muster, " that noe soldier may pretend ignorance." No power was reserved to the Sovereign by this statute to make articles of war. But in the first Mutiny Act passed in the reign of Queen Anne,* the right was saved to the Queen of making articles of war for the regulation of her forces beyond the seas in time of war; and in the 3rd of George I., and from that time to the present, Mutiny Acts have been annually passed giving the Sovereign power to make articles of war for the government of the troops generally, subject always to this limitation, that the punishment of death shall not be inflicted except in cases authorised by the Act. In each succeeding Act the preamble of the statute of William and Mary is repeated, and in each the great constitutional dogma is reasserted that " no man can be prejudged of life or limb, or subjected in time of peace† to any kind of punishment by martial law, or in any other

---

* 2 and 3 Anne, c. 20, sec. 37.

† These words, "in time of peace," occurring a second time in the preamble to the Act, are not in any of the Mutiny Acts prior to that of the 1st Anne. How they came to be introduced into that Act is not, I believe, known, but they have been repeated in every Mutiny Act since. Mr. Hopwood, in his able lecture on martial law, suggests that it may have happened through the oversight of the draftsman employed to draw the later Act, who, by inadvertence, repeated the words "in time of peace" a second time. —A. E. C.

manner than by judgment of his peers, and according to the known and established laws of the realm."

We have here a clear recognition of the principle that the Crown cannot legislate in time of peace even for the soldier. Assuredly there can be no greater power in respect of the civilian. But what is to be understood by the terms peace and war as occurring in these Acts? Are we to understand war to mean foreign war alone? or would it include a state of rebellion and intestine warfare? According to the authorities the criterion is whether the courts are open, and the course of justice uninterrupted.* Would then the Crown, in case of rebellion, have power to govern the army independently of the Mutiny Act— for instance, to declare offences capital which are not made so by the Mutiny Act? Would the Crown have power to place the subject under martial law? These are grave questions. Their solution is perhaps only to be found in a recurrence to first principles. It is certain that, while the Crown has (as we shall see presently) absolute power to legislate for the government of the army in time of war, though not, except under the Mutiny Acts, in time of peace, it has no power, whether in time of peace or time of war, to legislate in respect of the ordinary

---

* According to Lord Coke, "the time of peace is when the courts are open. For, when they are, you may have a commission of Oyer and Terminer, and where the common law can determine a thing, the martial law ought not." And again he says—"When the courts are open martial law cannot be executed" (3 Rushworth Collect., App., p. 81.) Lord Hale also says—"The exercise of martial law, whereby any person shall lose his life, or members, or liberty, may not be permitted in time of peace when the King's courts are open." Both these writers, it is to be ob-

subject. How, then, can the Sovereign have power to declare martial law as against the subject? For to declare martial law is to legislate. It is neither more nor less than to enact that the law of the land shall be for the time suspended, and a different law substituted for it. Whether this be effected by Act of Parliament, or by the proclamation of the Sovereign, it is equally legislation. How is this consistent with the indisputable principle that the Sovereign can only make laws in Parliament with the concurrence of the other estates of the realm? How is it consistent with the sacred principle of the Great Charter that no man shall be tried except by his peers and the law of the land?

But while principle and authority would thus appear to negative the power to declare martial law, it must be admitted that Parliament has, on more than one occasion, in the most distinct terms referred to it as an existing power. The Act of the 39th Geo. III., c. 11, to which I have already referred as passed by the Parliament of Ireland for the statutory exercise of

served, are speaking of martial law, not with reference to its exercise for the purpose of suppressing a rebellion, but as a rude substitute for the law of the land when, in time of war, justice cannot be administered by the ordinary tribunals. There is, however, I believe, no instance in English history in which the administration of justice has been suspended by reason of civil war. It certainly was not, according to Lord Coke, in the wars of Henry III., or during the Wars of the Roses, or during the great civil war. The distinction between "time of peace" and "time of war" is further discussed in the 1st Institute, p. 249 (a); not, however, with reference to martial law, but on the question as to the effect of a descent on the heir of a person seized of lands by occupation in time of war in taking away the right of entry of the true owner.—A. E. C.

martial law, among the recitals in the preamble states that "by the wise and salutary exercise of his Majesty's undoubted prerogative in executing martial law, for defeating and dispersing such armed and rebellious force, and in bringing divers rebels and traitors to punishment in the most speedy and summary manner, the peace of the kingdom has been so far restored as to permit the course of the common law partially to take place." The Act in question further contains the following proviso :—

"Provided always and be it declared and enacted, That nothing in this Act contained shall be construed to take away, abridge, or diminish the acknowledged prerogative of his Majesty for the public safety to resort to the exercise of martial law against open enemies or traitors, or any powers by law vested in the said Lord-Lieutenant or chief governor or governors of this kingdom, with or without the advice of his Majesty's Privy Council, or of any other person or persons whomsoever, to suppress treason and rebellion, and to do any act warranted by law for that purpose in the same manner as if this Act had never been made, or in any manner to call in question any Acts heretofore done for the like purposes."

Again, the Act of the United Parliament, the 43 Geo. III., c. 117, which has already been referred to, contains a reservation of what is therein stated to be the "undoubted prerogative" of the Crown, in the same terms as the Irish statute. And, again, the Act of the 3rd and 4th Wm. IV., c. 4, contains a similar reservation. The 40th section declares and enacts that "nothing in the Act contained shall be construed to take away, abridge, or diminish the undoubted prerogative of his Majesty for the public safety to resort to the exercise of martial law against open enemies or traitors."

We have to consider what is the effect of the recital
in the first of these statutes, and of the reservation of
the power of the Crown in that and the two later
ones. Now, there is an obvious difference between
the expression of the will of the legislature and the
expression of its opinion. When Parliament passes
an enacting statute—in other words, makes a law—
this exercise of its power is binding upon every one.
When, the law being doubtful, Parliament settles
the law by what is called a declaratory statute, this,
as coming from those who have power to make the
law, is considered as equivalent to an enactment. But
a recital or a reservation in a statute is a different
thing. Undoubtedly, if a statement of fact or of
law be recited as the foundation of legislation immediately following, such a recital is of the highest
authority; yet it is not conclusive. Even the collective
wisdom of the legislature is not always exempt from
the common liability to mistake. "A mere recital in
an Act of Parliament" (says Lord Campbell, in
delivering the judgment of the Court of Queen's
Bench in the case of the Queen against the inhabitants
of Haughton), "either of fact or of law, is not conclusive, and we are at liberty to consider the fact or
the law to be different from the statement in the
recital."* In the present instance, too, the effect of
the recital is greatly weakened by the fact that it was
wholly superfluous and unnecessary. The purpose of
reciting that by the exercise of martial law the rebellion
had been partly suppressed, whereby the ordinary
course of law had in some places been resumed,
of which persons guilty of treason had availed them-

* 1 Ellis and Blackburn's Reports, p. 516.

selves so as to avoid martial law, was all that was
necessary to found the enactment which was to follow
—namely, that the fact of the courts of law being open
should not prevent martial law from being put in force.
For this purpose it was perfectly indifferent whether
martial law was put in force by the power of the
Crown, or whether the power of the Crown was
"undoubted or not," and I do not think much weight
ought to be attached to a statement thus irregularly
and unnecessarily introduced.

Next, as to the effect of the reservations contained
in these statutes. Ordinarily speaking, the effect of
the reservation, in a statute, of any right or power is
not to affirm the existence of the right or power,
but simply to prevent the statute from having the
effect of impairing it if it exists. In the case of the
Lord Advocate v. Hamilton, in the House of Lords,*
where the Crown claimed the soil of the bed of a
public navigable river, which by an Act of Parliament
had been vested in trustees, on the ground that by
a saving clause the rights of the Crown had been
reserved, Lord Brougham said—"You cannot out
of this saving clause construe any right to be given
to the Crown. The right which the Crown had independently of it, and previously to it, is saved and
nothing more. The Crown is not to have its right
lessened or diminished; but nothing whatever is *given*
to the Crown by the saving clause, except the mode of
ascertaining its rights by petition to the Court of
Session. As, generally speaking, you cannot raise out
of a proviso or an exception in a statute any affirmative enactment, so you cannot, generally speaking,

* 1st Macqueen's Cases, p. 55.

raise out of a saving clause any affirmative or positive right whatever."

In the present instances, indeed, the legislature, in reserving the power, has described its existence as "acknowledged," or as "undoubted." So emphatic an expression of the opinion of Parliament is certainly entitled to great and respectful consideration; but in my opinion it cannot and ought not to prevail against fact and truth, if a thorough investigation of the subject should lead us to an opposite conclusion, and satisfy us that Parliament has formed an unsound opinion upon it. Against it may be set the fact that Parliament has passed Acts to indemnify persons who assisted in carrying martial law into execution, and took care to shut the doors of courts of law to those who would question its legality— enactments which would appear to have been wholly uncalled for, if the power to put martial law in force were as undoubted as it is thus described to be.*

Gentlemen, I have hitherto dealt with this subject entirely with reference to the general prerogative of

---

* There are those who, though satisfied of the illegality of martial law, hold nevertheless that a governor, or other officer invested with executive authority from the Crown, is bound, in case of necessity, to put martial law in force, and to trust to Parliament afterwards affording a statutory indemnity. To my mind, the exercise of martial law cannot be put on a worse or more objectionable footing. No man ought to be placed in the position of being called upon knowingly and intentionally to violate the law, more especially where the lives of his fellow-subjects are concerned; nor on any sound principle ought he to be protected if he does so. The only legitimate purpose of an Indemnity Act is to protect a man who, placed in trying circumstances, and called upon to exercise a doubtful and ill-defined power, has gone, as is very likely to happen

the Crown; but, as I said in the outset, it is possible that either by imperial or by local legislation a power may have been given to exercise this jurisdiction quite independent of any power derived from the Crown. Imperial legislation on the subject there is none; but there are one or two local statutes that are deserving of very serious attention with reference to this question. As I told you, the legislature of Jamaica, in the year 1680, acquired from the Crown power to make permanent statutes. Now, one of the first statutes made after that time was the Act of the 33rd of Charles II., chapter 21 (1682). It was an Act for establishing a militia in Jamaica. It was apprehended that the Spaniards, who were much dissatisfied at having lost the island, might attempt to recover it, or the Maroons in the mountains might be troublesome. There was no standing army in England from which troops could be spared for the defence of the island. It was therefore necessary to provide a military force which might be available in case of danger. I advert to these circumstances because they may throw some light on the enactments of the statute. It enacts, in the first place, that all persons from fifteen to sixty

in such a case, in ignorance or haste, but not intentionally, beyond the limits of the law. If the legality of martial law be doubtful, still more if the exercise of it be illegal, and it be deemed desirable that there should be power to resort to it in great emergencies, let that power be recognised or established by Parliament. But in that case, let us hope that the exercise of martial law will be placed under due limitations, and its administration fenced round by the safeguards which were wisely provided by the legislature in the Act of 1833. Without these it may well be doubted whether martial law is not, under any circumstances, a greater evil than that which it is intended to prevent.—A. E. C.

years of age shall be liable to bea◗ arms, and appoints
the arms and accoutrements with which they are to
furnish themselves. It provides for their being
mustered for a day, once in every two months,
in order to be drilled; and that while under arms
they are to "observe and keep all and every the
laws and articles of war, and to give due obedience
to their superior officers, and to the laws and articles
which the Commander-in-Chief, with the advice of the
council of war, is to make and establish." Then
comes a section* relating to martial law, which is in
these terms :—

"And be it further enacted that, upon every apprehension
and appearance of any public danger or invasion, the Commander-in-Chief shall forthwith call. a council of war, and,
with their advice and consent, cause and command the Articles
of War to be proclaimed at Port Royal and St. Jago de la
Vega. Upon which said publication the martial law is to be
in force."

Now the question that arises here is what is meant
by this expression, "from which said publication"—
that is, of the Articles of War—"the martial law is to
be in force." Observe what follows :—

"And then it shall and may be lawful for the said Commander-in-Chief to command the persons of any of his
Majesty's liege subjects, and also their negroes, horses, and
cattle, for all such service as may be for the public defence,
and to pull down houses, cut down timber, command ships
and boats, and generally to act and do with full power and
authority all such things as he and the said council of war
may think necessary and expedient for his Majesty's service
and the defence of this island. Provided always, and it is

* Sect. 7.

the true intent and meaning of this Act, that, as soon as the common law revives and is in force, the said negroes, horses, cattle, ships, and boats so employed be immediately discharged."

Then, "to the end that it may be certain when the martial law ceaseth and the common law revives and taketh place," provision is made that on the colours being lodged and the soldiers discharged, the martial law shall cease and the common law revive. The Act winds up with the following proviso :—

"Provided also, and it is hereby enacted and declared, that nothing within this Act or any clause therein contained shall be deemed, construed, or understood to give any captain-general or commander-in-chief any power or authority for the sending any person or persons off this island against their will, or to do any other act or thing contrary or repugnant to the known law of England or this island."

What, then, is the meaning of the words, "the martial law shall be in force?" One construction which it has been sought to put upon it, and which is the view propounded by the prosecution, is, that the martial law here to be put in force has reference to the militia alone. It must be remembered that the militia were not soldiers; they were the white inhabitants of the island, who were called upon by this statute to muster occasionally for the purpose of being drilled, but who, in ordinary times, were not embodied or kept on permanent duty. In the event, however, of the necessity arising, they were to be called out to take the field, and were then bound to serve till the danger had ceased. It is said, therefore, that "the martial law shall be in force" means simply that the militia force, as constituted by this Act, shall be bound to serve as soldiers, and be liable to military law. And it is contended with some show of reason that what immediately follows bears out this view. For the section immediately proceeds to enact, "that it shall then be lawful for the Commander-in-Chief to command the persons of any of his Majesty's liege subjects, and also their negroes, horses, and cattle, for all such service as may be for the public defence." So that this, it is contended, must be taken as the exposition of the martial law which the Governor is empowered to put in force. And in favour of this contention it must be borne in mind that, as appears from the language of Lord Coke and Lord Hale, the term martial law, as understood at that time, meant simply military law. Lastly, the final proviso of the statute must not be forgotten—namely, that no power is to be assumed to do anything contrary to the laws of England and of the island. Now, at this time the Petition of Right was, as I have already shown, applicable to Jamaica.

On the other hand, I must tell you that, since the passing of the Act to which I have just been calling your attention, the governors of the island, whether by virtue of this Act or of their commission I know not, appear to have been considered as possessing, not the limited power which would be contended for on the part of the prosecution, but full power to declare and exercise martial law in the amplest sense of the term, and that power seems to have been abundantly used.

I suppose there is no island or place in the world in which there has been so much of insurrection and disorder as the island of Jamaica. There is no place in which the curse which attaches to slavery, both as regards the master and the slave, has been more strikingly illustrated. Mr. Montgomery Martin, in his

history of the colonies, tells us, with reference to
Jamaica, that between the settlement of the colony
and the year 1832, a period of about 154 years, there
were no less than 28 insurrections of the negroes
in the island, being at the average rate of about one in
every five years and a-half, and these outbreaks appear
to have been put down with a degree of violence and
barbarity which is perfectly appalling. There were
two principal insurrections. One took place in the
year 1760, in which it is said that about 1,000 negroes
perished by execution and by slaughter of every kind,
and in which martial law was carried to an excess that
we perhaps never anywhere else heard of. If we may
believe the historians of the West Indies, speaking from
the narratives of eye-witnesses, not only was death
executed upon these unhappy negroes when driven into
revolt by the severity and cruelty to which they were
subject, but they were punished by the most unheard-
of barbarities, burning alive being one form of
executing these unfortunate wretches, while in some
instances care was taken that the torture should be
prolonged to the last possible moment. Another great
rebellion occurred in the years 1831 and 1832, and
though similar atrocities were not perpetrated then,
yet a vast number of executions and of other punishments took place. Now, if this power of putting
martial law in force was exercised by virtue of this
statute, we have not only a contemporaneous exposition, always a matter of importance in interpreting
a doubtful statute, but we have an exposition of it
by the practice of two centuries. But it may be
that the power was exercised by the governors as
inherent in the authority given by their commissions;

nor ought we to overlook the fact that it was the exercise by the powerful of what law they pleased upon those who were entirely at their mercy, and upon whom they were desirous of inflicting the speediest and the direst vengeance.

There is another statute of the Jamaica legislature which is very important, and which certainly goes much further than the one I have just been referring to—an Act passed as late as the ninth year of the Queen. This also is a Militia Act. This Act undoubtedly recognises martial law, and recognises it to the fullest extent. It is not like the former Act, in which the term martial law is capable of being interpreted by reference to what was then known in England under that name, or by words which follow as limiting the power which the Governor was to exercise; but it appears to deal with martial law in the largest sense. The 96th section of this Act is as follows:—"And whereas the appearance of public danger by invasion or otherwise may sometimes make the imposition of martial law necessary, yet, as from experience of the mischiefs and calamities attending it, it must ever be considered as among the greatest of evils"—Well indeed might they say so, for there is not a stone in that island of Jamaica, that, if the rains of Heaven had not washed off from it the stains of blood, might not have borne terrible witness to this sad truth!—It then goes on—"Be it therefore enacted, That it shall not in future be declared or imposed but by the opinion or advice of a council of war consisting as aforesaid." Now, it is true, this is in one sense a restraining statute. It takes away from the Governor the power to proclaim martial law except upon a given condition; it subjects his authority in that respect to the assent of a council of war to be summoned for the purpose. But then, upon the other hand, it plainly indicates that the exercise of martial law is considered as within the province of the Governor, and from the painful language of the recital, it appears that martial law is spoken of, not in its application to military offences by military tribunals, but as it had previously been applied in the island in cases of public disturbance. Therefore, this statute is one which deserves very serious consideration in determining the question whether the Governor has or has not, by statutory enactment, the power to declare martial law even if he had it not by virtue of his authority derived from the Crown.*

* Since the delivery of this charge, I have perused with great interest a paper recently written by Mr. Phillippo, the Jamaica barrister, on the subject of martial law in Jamaica, in which he passes in review the whole of the local legislation on the subject of the militia, and sets forth the series of historical facts which are necessary for the proper understanding of these Acts with reference to the question of martial law. According to his view, I was wrong in ascribing to the term martial law in the modern statute of the 9th Victoria any larger meaning than attaches to it in the first Militia Act of the 33rd Charles II.; as also in thinking that martial law had been applied to the negro population when in a state of rebellion. Mr. Phillippo fully develops the argument that the term martial law in the first statute simply means that which, in modern phraseology, is called military law, and that it had reference to the militia alone. He urges that the purpose of the enactment was to enable the Governor to subject the free population of the island, when converted into soldiers for its defence, to military law, without which the force could not have been managed and controlled; and he observes, most correctly, that the term "martial law," or "law martial," was the only one used in that day to designate the law by which the soldier was governed. It may be worth while to men-

Assuming the existence of the power to put martial law in force, whether as inherent in the prerogative or as derived from statutory enactment, a question of vital

tion, in confirmation of this view, that Lord Belmore, the then Governor of Jamaica, in a despatch, dated January 6, 1832, addressed to Lord Goderich, mentions, as one of the reasons which had induced him to proclaim martial law, that "by that means alone he could obtain complete control over the militia force, on whose services he must chiefly depend to put down the rebellion." —"Parliamentary Papers," Vol. XXXVII.

Mr. Phillippo next denies that martial law was applied to the revolted negro. The slaves had no civil rights; they could not claim to be tried before the regular tribunals, or according to the common law. If they revolted they were subdued and put to death under the provisions of statutes which were called in Jamaica "Party" Acts, so called because they provided for the formation of parties, from those liable to serve in the militia, to pursue and destroy runaway or revolted slaves. "It was under the Party Acts," says Mr. Phillippo, agreeing in the fact of the horrible barbarities inflicted on the blacks, "that the cruelties were perpetrated. There are a great number of them on the statute book, enforcing parties from the militia, encouraging voluntary parties of free blacks, Maroons, and even of confidential slaves, to go out against rebellious or runaway negroes, without declaring martial law, which it is said, in the language of one of the Acts, 'cannot be declared without many and great inconveniences to this island in general, and ought not to be declared but in cases of the most urgent necessity.' The first of these Acts is the 11th William III., c. 1, and some of them continued in force until the abolition of slavery. By these Acts the parties got so much for each negro killed, some of them requiring the head or ears of such negro as vouchers, and a somewhat larger amount for each negro brought in alive (£15 for the killed and £20 for the captured, and all the plunder in some instances). Those brought in alive were liable to be tried under the slave Court. The punishments inflicted, by the earlier Slave Courts at least, were positively barbarous."

"During the last insurrection in Jamaica in 1831," continues Mr. Phillippo, "and prior to the abolition of slavery, these laws were in force. All the free male persons, from 15 to 60, were in the militia,

importance presents itself, namely, What is this martial
law which is thus to supersede the common law of
England? And here, again, on entering on this branch

and upon martial law being declared were subject to military law.
The Maroons were also, under their own organisation, subject to
military law. The slaves were in armed insurrection, and had some
engagements with the military. Courts-martial did sit upon them,
and pass sentence on them; but they had no civil rights further than
was granted to them very imperfectly by the Slave Acts. They had
forfeited their lives by rising in insurrection; the military authorities were at liberty to shoot them down, or to take them prisoners.
If they chose to try them by court-martial, they were con-
travening no English legislation or doctrine of English common
law. The slave had no civil rights, except such as had been
grudgingly given by the Slave Acts, and if those were contravened,
it was rather for the master to complain than the slave. Some free
persons would also seem to have been apprehended, but an Act
of Indemnity was applied for and obtained (2nd William IV.,
c. 25). The free people at that time would, of course, be enrolled
in the militia, or liable to serve; indeed, many even of the mis-
sionaries were compelled to do military duty, and all in the militia
were subject to military law."

With regard to the recital in the 96th section of the 9th of
Victoria, chapter 35, Mr. Phillippo maintains that the mention of
"the mischief and calamities" attending the imposition of martial
law therein has no reference to those which fall on the unhappy
population who become its victims, but to the white population,
who, on the proclamation of martial law, were compelled to leave
their affairs and their homes, and serve in the field under the
rigour of military discipline. And this view is strongly confirmed
by the similar recital in one of the "Party" Acts referred to by
Mr. Phillippo. So that the reference to martial law in the later
statute amounts to no recognition of any power in the Governor to
enforce any other martial law than was contemplated by the first
statute.

I regret that from want of space I am not enabled to give the
whole of this interesting and able paper, which will, however, I
hope, see the light in some form or other.

I am strongly disposed to think that Mr. Phillippo makes good

of the inquiry, it becomes necessary to eliminate from
the discussion matters which are in reality foreign to it.
I have already adverted to the fact that the execution
of persons taken in arms, or taken in pursuit, and put
to death as rebels, is not in question here. But there
are other things, also, which have been confounded
with martial law which I think it essential to separate
from it. A distinguished authority,* while maintaining that martial law, being founded on necessity, was
therefore a law which was to be expanded to any
extent commensurate with the necessity of the case,
says, " You surely do not mean to say that if a mutiny
breaks out on board a ship, or in the army, you are to
have recourse to the ordinary tribunals of the country,
and the ordinary law of the country, in such a
case ?" Certainly not : but it is to my mind a serious
mistake to suppose that this is any part of martial law
—especially of martial law as it is propounded for the
present purpose. It is simply the application of a universally acknowledged principle ; namely, that where
illegal force is resorted to for the purpose of crime,

both his propositions : 1st, that the term martial law used in these
statutes means simply the law in force in the army ; 2ndly, that
the power given to the Governor to call that law into operation
has reference only to the militia, so as to enable him to subject
them to military discipline under that law, when circumstances
rendered it necessary that they should be embodied and take the
field. If this be so, these Acts would give no power to the Governor
to put martial law in force against insurgents, and the existence of
such a power must, therefore, depend entirely on whether it is conferred, expressly or impliedly—and in point of law can be conferred
—by his commission.—A. E. C.

* Sir David Dundas, Judge Advocate General, before the Ceylon
Committee.

you may meet that illegal force by force, and may
repress and prevent it by any amount of force that
may be necessary for the purpose, even if that necessity should involve the death of the offender. If a
man attacks you with intention to murder you, or to
do you bodily harm ; if a man stops you on the high-
way to rob you ; if he invades the sanctity of your
dwelling by night, under circumstances calculated to
inspire you with apprehension and fear, you are not
bound to submit to the injury that may presently be
done you, and to leave it to the law afterwards to
avenge the wrong : you may at once take the law into
your own hands (to use a popular expression), and in
self-protection, or for the prevention of crime, kill the
offender by any means in your power. In like manner,
if a mutiny breaks out on board ship, immediate force
may be resorted to ; you may quell the mutiny if necessary by killing those engaged in it. So, if a regiment
in an army, or a company in a regiment, breaks out
into mutiny, you may put it down at once by the
immediate application of force. You may order other
troops to fire on them, or put them to the sword, if
they refuse to submit. But this is not what can properly be called martial law. It is part and parcel of
the law of England—or perhaps I should say it is a
right paramount to all law, and which the law of every
civilised country recognises—that life may be protected or crime prevented by the immediate application of any amount of force which, under the circumstances, may be necessary. But that is not what we
are now dealing with. What we are considering is
whether, for the suppression of a rebellion, you may
subject persons not actively engaged in it, and whom

you therefore cannot kill on the spot, to an anomalous
and exceptional law, and try them for their lives
without the safeguards which the law ought to afford.
We may therefore dismiss the cases in which it is permitted to put men to death without process of law, as
altogether foreign to the purpose, and come back to
the question as to what martial law in the proper sense
of the term really is.

Two views are put forward : the one that martial
law applied to the civil subject is neither more nor
less than the law applicable to the soldier applied to
the civilian. Thus it was said in Parliament some
years ago by one of the great men* of our time that
assuming that the proclamation of martial law could
affect civilians, the effect of it would be to place every
man in the position of a soldier. The other is, that
while the law martial—as Coke, and Hale, and Blackstone call it—or, as it is the fashion now-a-days to
term it, the military law—as applicable to the soldier,
is a precise, ascertained, and well-defined law, martial
law, when applied to the civilian, is no law at all, but
a shadowy, uncertain, precarious something, depending
entirely on the conscience, or rather on the despotic
and arbitrary will, of those who administer it. Here,
again, let us see whether we can obtain assistance from
history towards the solution of the question. Let us
see what has been the only martial law heretofore
known in England, namely, the law applicable to military duties and offences.

It is obvious that when a body of armed men are

* Lord (then Mr.) Brougham on the debate in the House of
Commons on the case of Mr. Smith, the missionary, who had been
subjected to martial law in Demerara. See "Hansard," vol. xi., p. 990.

brought together for military purposes, a special law is necessary for their government and control. Not only the efficiency but the safety of an army depends upon the maintenance of strict subordination and discipline. Moreover, when you bring together a body of men in the vigour of life, generally men of determined spirit (for those are the men who are most prone to seek military service), who from the consciousness of having arms in their hands may feel their superiority to the ordinary population with whom they are brought into contact, a special law is required for the purpose of keeping these persons in proper subjection and order. And, looking to the serious consequences which may ensue from military offences, especially from breaches of duty or discipline, a more speedy and summary process than is required in the case of offenders against the ordinary law may doubtless be necessary; and as the offences against military duty are generally simple and easily capable of proof, a more speedy process may be justifiable than in the trial of offences against the ordinary law has been found by experience compatible with the safe administration of justice. Such law there has undoubtedly been from the earliest times, and that law has emanated from the Sovereign. For, from the earliest period—at all events from the Norman Conquest, and we need not go back beyond that—it has always, except in the short period of the civil war in the time of Charles I., been acknowledged that the government of the army was in the absolute power of the Sovereign. Whatever restraint the power of the Barons, or, at a later period, the sturdy assertion of popular rights by the Commons of

England, may have placed on the power of the Crown, with that one exception no one has ever denied that it was for the Sovereign to make those laws which should be specially applicable to the military forces as distinguished from the rest of the community. Accordingly, from a very early period, we find, upon the occasion of armies being collected, the Sovereigns of this country making laws and ordinances for the government of their soldiers. In those days there was no standing army. When the King had occasion to go to war, he summoned the feudatories, who were bound by the tenure of their estates to serve in war, and at a later period the array of each county, when it had been settled by statute that every man who held land was bound to provide arms and serve in the field, and lastly, any mercenaries whom his means enabled him to engage. Collected for the particular war, when the war was over the army was disbanded; but for its government while it remained in arms the King made laws and ordinances. Lord Hale says— "Always, preparatory to an actual war, the Kings of this realm, by the advice of the Constable and Marshal, were used to compose a book of rules and orders for the due order and discipline of their officers and soldiers, together with certain penalties upon the offenders, and this was called *martial law;* and we have extant in the Black Book of the Admiralty, and elsewhere, several examples of such military laws, and especially that of Richard II., composed by the King with the advice of the Duke of Lancaster and others."* I have not, Gentlemen, referred to

* Hale, "History of the Common Law," p. 34.

the book at the Admiralty, but I find in other public acts and documents of this country and other sources of information a succession of these ordinances for the government of the army, emanating always from the Royal authority. Lord Hale refers to the ordinance of Richard II., but there are earlier ones than that. There is an ordinance of Richard I., on the occasion of his departure by sea for the Holy Land. His laws are short, but remarkable for the excessive severity of the punishments which are to be inflicted. If a man commits a murder at sea, he is to be tied to the body of the dead man and thrown into the sea; if he commits a murder on shore, he is to be tied to the body of the dead man and buried alive; if a man steals from his comrade he is to have his head shorn, and boiling pitch is to be poured on it, and in that condition he is to be landed and left to take his chance.*

There are constitutions of King John for the government of the army. No laws or ordinances of Henry III. or of the Edwards, so far as I am aware, have come down to us. The next we have are those of Richard II., preserved in the Cottonian MSS. in the British Museum, and entitled, " Statutes, Ordonnances, and Customs to be observed in the Army." These statutes are very remarkable. They form an elaborate code, minute in its details to a degree that might serve as a model to anybody drawing up a code of criminal law. They follow the soldier into every department of military life and service. They point out his duty to his officers, his duties to the service, his duties to

* Rymer's "Fœdera," vol. i., p. 65.

his comrades, his duties with regard to the unarmed population with whom he may come in contact. They show what would be infractions of these duties, and attach specific penalties to every violation of the law so set forth. I will not take you through these ordinances—it would occupy too much time; it is sufficient to state the general character of them. As we advance in history we find others equally elaborate, equally specific and precise. King Henry V. issued several such ordinances which have come down to us. On the occasion of his invading France he published an elaborate set of ordinances.* He did the same for the government of his garrison in the town of Rouen, and other places in France.† The next we have are of the reign of Henry VII.,‡ when he mustered his army to go against the rebel forces in the North, which ended in the battle of Stoke, to which I have already reverted. And, lastly, we have a series of ordinances and statutes published by King Henry VIII.,§ when he meditated an invasion of France. These, like the others, are elaborate, minute, and particular to the greatest possible degree, pointing out all the duties of the soldier, and all the offences of which a soldier's life may be capable, even to the irregularities which may interfere with his duty, and specifying the punishments which were to follow on the infraction of the law.

We have not, that I am aware of, any statutes or ordinances of the next ensuing reigns. I suppose by

---

* See Grose's "Military Antiquities," vol. ii., p. 66.

† These are to be found in the 10th vol. of Rymer, p. 106.

‡ Leland's "Collectanea," vol. iv., p. 213.

§ Preserved in the College of Arms.

this time the military law, through this succession of ordinances, had become tolerably fixed and settled, and had acquired, as all other law does by the force of custom, the validity which custom gives. But in the commencement of the civil wars in the time of Charles I. we find these ordinances coming up again. When the Scottish army invaded England, the generals published ordinances for the guidance and rule of the soldier, very much of the same description as those which had been published in the time of King Henry VIII.* The Earl of Northumberland, on the other hand, commanding the King's forces, issued his ordinances. When the civil war broke out, the Earl of Essex issued an equally elaborate body of laws for the government of his forces.† In the reign of James II. we have the same thing under the same form and name as we have it now—namely, Articles of War; and those Articles of War are substantially the Articles of War which we have now. Then come the Mutiny Acts and Articles of War periodically issued by the Sovereign for the government of the forces of this realm; and any one who has taken the trouble to look into the Articles of War by which the army is governed, must, I think, do those who framed them the justice to say that they are most elaborate and precise, and that it is impossible for any one who takes any trouble to ascertain his duty, and the penalties which attach to the breach of it, not to be perfectly aware of the law by which he is to be governed.

Such is the military law. There is nothing arbitrary or uncertain in it. It is precise, specific, definite.

---

* They are given at length in Grose, u. s., p. 85.
† Ib., p. 107.

It is, in short, so far as it goes, all that can be wanted. So much for the substantive law. • Now let us look at what may be called the ancillary law; that is, the judicature and forms of procedure by which the law is to be enforced.

From the earliest period of our history the military law has been administered by competent tribunals under an ascertained and regulated mode of procedure. As early as the reign of William the Conqueror, when the judicature of this country was settled upon the footing on which it has in great measure remained to the present hour—when the great Aula Regia was established, with the various branches of judicature which it contained—the Marshal's Court, as it was called—that is, the Court of the High Constable and the Earl Marshal of England—was instituted, and was as much part of the settled and established judicature of the country as the Courts of Queen's Bench, Common Pleas, or Exchequer; and by these great officers, and their deputies and assistants, the military law was administered. They always attended the King in his wars; the High Constable of England being the general who commanded under the King, the Earl Marshal being his deputy, next in rank and authority, and whose province it was to muster and marshal the army, and to regulate its internal economy. These great officers held a court of war for the trial of all military delinquencies and their punishment. They had also a court in this country which had jurisdiction over high treason and offences committed abroad (except on the high seas, in which case offences fell under the jurisdiction of the admiral), and for the trial of all things relating to arms or honour.

This court had encroached at an early period on the common law, which caused the passing of the statute of the 13 Rich. II., c. 2, for the purpose of fixing the precise limits of its jurisdiction. That statute runs thus :—

"*Item.*—Because the commons do make a grievous complaint that the court of the constable and the marshal hath incroached to him, and daily doth incroach contracts, covenants, trespasses, debts, and detinues, and many other actions pleadable at the common law, in great prejudice of the King and of his courts, and to the great grievance and oppression of the people; our lord the King, willing to ordain a remedy against the prejudices and grievances aforesaid, hath declared in this parliament, by the advice and assent of the lords spiritual and temporal, the power and jurisdiction of the said constable, in the form that followeth :—To the constable it pertaineth to have cognizance of contracts touching deeds of arms and of war out of the realm, and also of things that touch war within the realm, which cannot be determined nor discussed by the common law, with other usages and customs to the same matters pertaining, which other constables heretofore have duly and reasonably used in their time."

This court had its regular officers, its pursuivants, its heralds, and other inferior ministers; and it acted partly by the civil law, as it is said (by which I suppose the old writers mean the law of the continent, because the civil law, that is, the Roman law, properly so called, says nothing about military procedure at all).* In some respects they adopted the law of England, certainly in some of its most essential particulars. The procedure of this court was from an early period fixed and settled, and has continued so to the present hour. At this day the

---

* See Digest, lib. 49, tit. 16 de re militari.

procedure of the military courts is a perfectly understood and established thing, derived, as far as I can
judge, from the old procedure of the court of the
High Constable and the Earl Marshal of England.
These great officers continued to administer justice in
all military matters down to the time of Henry VIII.
That monarch, jealous of authority, was dissatisfied at
having so great an officer as the High Constable near
the throne, the office being hereditary, and the
Constable entitled to command the armies under
the King; and as it happened that the Duke of
Buckingham, who was the High Constable of England
in that reign, was attainted of high treason and executed, the King took advantage of his death, and did
not appoint another; and from that time the office of
the High Constable of England has been disused.
The Earl Marshal continued, however, to exercise
jurisdiction in the army as before, and this continued
until the time of King Charles I. In the time of
James I., indeed, a question was raised whether, as
the office of the High Constable no longer existed,
the Earl Marshal by himself was competent to exercise
jurisdiction in matters of military cognisance where
questions of life or death were involved. The Lord
Keeper, the Master of the Rolls, and the Privy Council at that time held that the Earl Marshal's jurisdiction was not put an end to by reason of the non-
existence of his coadjutor, the High Constable, and
the court continued for a time; but in the subsequent
reign, the same question having again been raised, the
Judges were of opinion that the Earl Marshal had not
jurisdiction without the High Constable, and from that
time the jurisdiction of the Earl Marshal in criminal

matters was discontinued, and the court abolished. Hereupon, as it was of course necessary that there should be some tribunal to adjudicate in matters of military cognisance, the course pursued seems to have been, as far as one can judge from the ordinances of the Earl of Essex, that a council of war was appointed, while the army was in the field, as also an officer called the "General Marshal;" for this officer is mentioned in those ordinances as the person who, with the council of war, would have to determine questions of military-delinquency. But it seems that this office was soon superseded, and courts-martial introduced, in its stead, for the trial of military offences, in the manner in which courts-martial are appointed at the present day, and so the law has remained.

As I have said, the procedure appears from the earliest time to have been regular, and when the ancient and established court was superseded or got rid of, and courts-martial were substituted in its place, it would appear that these courts-martial adopted the procedure of the old military court of the Constable and Earl Marshal; for it is to this day a mixed procedure, as it is described to have been by the old writers; a procedure in which some of the technicalities of the common law are dispensed with,* and a different mode of proceeding is adopted, but in which trials are conducted according to fixed and established rules, rules which appear to have existed from the earliest times.

* The great advantage of the military procedure appears to be that it avoids the delays incidental to our system of administering justice periodically, so that punishment follows speedily upon crime, and so operates more effectually to deter.—A. E. C.

We have not, however, quite done with the subject of military tribunals. There are two forms of proceeding, which are of a more irregular and exceptional character, and which may have contributed to acquire for martial law the character which some people ascribe to it. When an army was on the march or in the field, there used to be—there is not, I believe, any longer—a proceeding called a drum-head court-martial. If a man was taken almost or quite in the fact of committing a military offence—or as they term it, red-handed—and it was desirable to make an immediate example, as in the case of mutiny or plunder, or the like, it was the practice to bring him—there not being time or means to constitute a proper court, or to conduct the trial with the usual formalities—before a court collected on the spot, and called a drum-head court-martial, because, as the old writers say, the proceedings were written on the head of the drum. The guilt of the offender being flagrant and apparent, this short and summary proceeding was thought sufficient, and the man was immediately punished. This was certainly a much nearer approach to what is now called martial law than anything that took place in the ordinary course of military trials. That system has, however, I believe, fallen into disuse. I see in one of the late works on martial law, *Hough's Precedents*, that officers have even been brought before courts-martial in later years for resorting to these drum-head courts-martial. The 11th section of the Mutiny Act has, however, provided a proceeding of a somewhat analogous character. It enacts that—

"In cases of mutiny and gross insubordination, or other offences committed on the line of march, or on board any transport-ship, convict-ship, merchant vessel, or troop-ship, not in commission, the offender may be tried by a regimental or detachment court-martial, and the sentence may be confirmed and carried into execution on the spot by the officer in the immediate command of the troops; provided that the sentence shall not exceed that which a regimental court-martial is competent to award."

Such a court would not, therefore, have authority to pass sentence of death, this being beyond the power of a regimental court-martial. Besides this, there always has been, in our armies, an officer called a Provost-Marshal. The Articles of War require the appointment of such an officer, and his duties and functions are pointed out very clearly.* With his assistants, he exercises, as it were, the police of an army on the march or in the field. He is to be perpetually moving about the camp, to see that no offences or excesses are committed; and if he himself catches a man in the act of committing a military offence, he has authority summarily to punish him on the spot, according to the exigency of the case, applying the punishment which might be awarded by sentence of a court-martial if the man had been regularly brought to trial; but his jurisdiction in this respect is exclusively confined to delinquencies which he himself catches the offender in the act of committing, and as to which, therefore, a trial would be unnecessary. Here, again, this very summary jurisdiction may have led to mistaken notions on the subject of martial law.

Setting aside these two exceptional modes of proceeding, although doubtless the procedure of courts-

* Article 161.

G

martial is capable of considerable amendment, no one, I think, can deny that the substance of justice is carefully attended to. There is nothing arbitrary, nothing capricious, nothing unsettled. The charge must be distinctly specified; the evidence must be such as any ordinary court of justice would receive; the accused has the fullest opportunity of defence; the witnesses must be confronted with him; he has the opportunity of cross-examination — much impaired, it must be admitted, by the mode in which it is carried on —yet still affording the opportunity of having such questions put to the witnesses as he may desire; he has the fullest opportunity of being heard; he has the right to call such witnesses as he may think fit. It is true he has not the advantage—the inestimable advantage, I think it—of having his case advocated by those who are practised in the science and skill of advocacy, and who know how to bring out everything that can possibly make for the benefit of the client, whereby in the end truth is elicited by all that can be said on either side being heard, and the tribunal which has to judge is placed in the most advantageous position for deciding according to right. This, no doubt, is wanting. But we must not forget that, until a very recent period, however ignorant, however humble, however timid, however incompetent to grapple with the difficulties of his case, a person standing upon his trial for life or death had no opportunity of having an advocate to speak on his behalf. Happily that state of things, which arose in a time of benighted and barbarous ignorance, has passed away, and possibly the day is not far off when this defect in the procedure of military tribunals, as well as the defective method of cross-examination, will be amended. On the other hand, we cannot doubt that the substance of justice is carefully attended to, and perhaps there are no tribunals in the world in which justice is administered with a higher sense of the obligation which the exercise of judicial functions imposes, with a higher sense of honour, or a greater desire to do justice. These, I think, so far as experience has shown, are, generally speaking, the characteristics of the military tribunals which exercise their functions under the name of courts-martial.

Now, if such be the law as applied to the soldier, why should it not be the law applicable to the civilian? Why are we to be told that when you come to deal with a civilian by martial law, it is to be something different from the martial law which is applied to the soldier? I confess myself at a loss for any reason that can be given for that assertion, and certainly before I adopt the doctrine that a law, if it may be called a law, of the uncertain and arbitrary character which martial law is said to be, can be administered in this country, and that Englishmen can be tried for their lives under it, I shall require something more than assertion unsupported by authority. Of this I am perfectly sure—namely, that in those repertories of the law of England which have been compiled by the sages and fathers of the law, and which have been handed down to us with the sanction of their great names, to inform us, and those who are to come after us in future ages, what the law of England was and is, no authority for anything of the sort can be found. On the contrary, when Coke, and Hale, and Blackstone speak of martial law, it is plain they are speaking of the law applicable to the soldier, or what in modern phrase is called military law. It is plain that they knew of no other; and the fact that when speaking, and clearly speaking, about the law applicable to soldiers, such men as Lord Hale and Sir William Blackstone, with their accuracy of statement, call it martial law, and do not point out any distinction between martial law and military law as it is spoken of now, goes far indeed to show that they knew of no such difference, and that the distinction now supposed to exist is a thing that has come into the minds of men certainly much later than when those eminent luminaries of the law of England wrote their celebrated treatises.

On the other hand, let us see what authority there is which justifies the assertion that, if martial law can be legally exercised, it can be exercised in the arbitrary and despotic form which some persons contend for, as being something that has no limit, except the particular exigency, or, I might almost say, the convenience of the moment. I will bring before you all that I have been enabled to discover. In the first place, I find this distinction taken in the works upon military courts-martial, written mostly by military men, as I think, from an entire misconception of the meaning of Lord Hale, and especially of that of Sir William Blackstone in his Commentaries—a work probably more ready to their hands, and the language of which is certainly ambiguous and calculated to mislead until you carefully look to see what is the subject-matter of which he is treating, upon which all difficulty vanishes. But military writers upon courts-martial certainly do make this distinction, and there is also the authority of two distinguished members of

the legal profession, though not of judicial position.
Mr. Headlam, certainly a gentleman of great learning
and judgment, being called upon, when Judge-Advocate General, to afford information to the commissioners at that time appointed under a Royal Commission to inquire into the defences of the United
Kingdom, makes the following statement. He writes—

"I have to observe, with a view of preventing any mis-
understanding on the subject, that there is a broad distinction
between the martial law called into existence and the law
administered by courts-martial for the ordinary government
of the army, which for distinction and accuracy may be called
'military law.' The latter, namely, military law, is applicable
only to the army and such other persons connected with it as
are made amenable to it by the Mutiny Act. Martial law,
according to the Duke of Wellington, is 'neither more nor
less than the will of the general who commands the army; in
fact, martial law means no law at all. Therefore the general
who declares martial law, and commands that it shall be carried
into execution, is bound to lay down the rules, regulations, and
limits, according to which his will is to be carried out.' "

The opinion thus cited by Mr. Headlam was that of
a very great man, and as to what may be done in an
enemy's country, in time of war, may be perfectly sound
—on that I pronounce no opinion—but I cannot accept
the opinion even of so great a man as authority on a
question of law, and I certainly should not recommend
anybody to act upon it in case martial law should
be proclaimed in our own country, or to rely on
it as a protection if called upon to answer for his
conduct in a court of justice for any injury inflicted on
a fellow-subject in the exercise of martial law. Mr.
Headlam goes on to say—

"The effect of the proclamation of martial law in a district of England is a notice to the inhabitants that the executive Government has taken upon itself the responsibility of superseding the jurisdiction of all the ordinary tribunals, for the protection of life, person, and property, and has authorised the military authorities to do whatever they think expedient for the public safety."*

All this may be true, but I should like to know on what authority this statement rests. I can only say that I have not been able to find it, and I hope I shall give no offence when I say that, in a matter of such importance, before such doctrines as these, involving such serious consequences if carried into effect, are enunciated in this positive and unqualified manner, and spoken of as though of ordinary occurrence, some judicial decision or some high legal authority should be cited, or at all events instances adduced of the exercise of such a power.

I have also to call attention to the opinion of a gentleman, for whose great learning, accomplished mind, and sound judgment I have the greatest respect, and to whose opinion I should certainly be disposed to pay great deference—I mean Sir David Dundas, who, being then Judge Advocate-General, on being examined before the Committee upon the events that had taken place in Ceylon, certainly lays down much the same doctrine. He says that "the proclamation of martial law is a notice to all those to whom the proclamation is addressed that there is another measure of law and another mode of proceeding than there was before;" that "where martial law is proclaimed, there is no rule or law by which the officers executing

* Report of Commissioners appointed to consider the defences of the United Kingdom, Appendix, p. 90.

it are bound;" "that it is more extensive than ordinary military law;" that "it overrides all other law, and that it is entirely arbitrary." Here, again, I must say I am struck with the absence of any authority for so sweeping, and, to my mind, so strong an assertion. At the same time, I must do Sir David Dundas the justice to add that, with characteristic candour, he took care to inform the Committee that martial law was a matter on which he had no special knowledge, because it did not come at all within the sphere of his official duty. The same observation applies to Mr. Headlam. As Sir David Dundas pointed out, the Judge Advocate-General has only to deal with matters that come under the exercise of the ordinary military law and the ordinary military tribunals, and there is nothing to bring the subject of martial law under his particular attention, or to lead him to devote any special research to the question of what martial law, as distinguished from military law, is. His province ceases where the military law ends, and he has nothing to do with any other, and therefore does not know more about it than any one else. I advert to this because it might otherwise be thought that a Judge Advocate-General must, from his office, have a special knowledge on such a matter.

To these authorities should be added the opinion of two distinguished judicial personages, Lord Cottenham and Lord Campbell, given extra-judicially, it is true, yet still, as coming from such men, entitled to respectful consideration. It was stated by Earl Grey in the House of Lords, on the debate on the affairs of Ceylon, in April, 1851, that those two noble and learned Lords, as also Sir John Jervis, when Attorney-General, had advised him, when Secretary of State, very much to the effect of what is stated in the opinions already referred to. This opinion was, however, as I have already observed, entirely extra-judicial, and probably was given without much consideration. Nor has the subject of martial law been discussed before an English Court since the case of Grant *v.* Gould, in 1794. Here, again, therefore, I am at a loss to know upon what authority these expressions of opinion are founded.

Whence, then, has arisen this doctrine as to the distinction between martial and military law, unknown, as it evidently was, to our great legal writers? Partly, I think, from the loose language of historians, who, when they speak of rebels or insurgents put to death without trial, are apt to apply the term martial law to such summary proceedings. Partly from the reckless assertions of Hume, too long the oracle of a credulous public, who describes martial law as "a prompt, arbitrary, and violent method of decision," and who, without the shadow of authority, boldly affirms that "under it any one might be punished as a rebel, or an aider and abettor in rebellion, whom the provost-marshal or lieutenant of a county, or their deputies, pleased to suspect." Partly from the inaccurate language even of Hale and Blackstone themselves. For when, speaking of martial law, Lord Hale describes it "as in truth and reality not a law, but something indulged rather than allowed as a law;"* and especially when Sir William Blackstone in his Commentaries says that martial law "is built upon no

* "History of the Common Law," p. 34.

settled principles, but is entirely arbitrary in its decisions,"* people might well run away with the notion that this language was applicable to martial law when exercised in the heat and hurry of intestine troubles. Nothing, however, can be clearer, when the context is carefully looked at, than that both these writers were speaking of the law applicable to the soldier, for which, in their day, the term martial law or law martial was the only designation in use.†

But nothing, I apprehend, has so much contributed to foster the opinion that martial law must be arbitrary, despotic, and absolved from all legal rule, as the excesses and abuses which have been committed in the exercise of this power. And in this respect Jamaica

---

* "Commentaries," vol. i., p. 413.

† Mr. Tytler (Judge-Advocate of Scotland, and afterwards a Lord of Session under the title of Lord Woodhouselee), in his "Essay on Military Law and Practice of Courts-Martial," has with great pains, and not without some heat, vindicated the military law from these animadversions of Lord Hale and Sir William Blackstone, asserting that "the principles of military law are as certain, determinate, and immutable as the principles of the common or statutory law which regulate the civil classes of society." The fact is that probably neither Hale nor Blackstone, though profoundly versed in knowledge of the law of England, knew much about the law martial, which had not then, I believe, been made the subject of any distinct work or treatise; besides which, these great lawyers, wedded and devoted to the common law, the study of their lives, would be very apt to look with utter contempt on a law administered by military tribunals, and refuse to acknowledge it as law at all. The history of military law, which I have already traced, sufficiently shows that Hale and Blackstone were wrong in treating martial law as the purely arbitrary and lawless system which they represent it. But what they have said of it as applicable to the soldier would be quite true of it as applied to the civilian, if the modern doctrine is to be maintained.—A. E. C.

itself may have contributed to the result, with its summary executions and slaughter of negroes, coupled with proclamations of martial law, whatever may have been the purpose of the latter. The manner, too, in which, in the midst of tumult and passion, martial law was executed in Ireland at the close of the last century, had probably much to do in developing the prevailing notions about martial law. That great excesses were then committed it seems impossible to doubt. Even before martial law was proclaimed, the magistrates themselves, as appears from the periodical Indemnity Acts, committed flagrant violations of the law in dealing with persons supposed to be disaffected. We can easily imagine what would be likely to happen when the proclamation of Lord Camden had handed over the population to the militia and yeomanry. One of the first acts of Lord Cornwallis, on assuming the office of Lord-Lieutenant in the course of 1798, was to interfere to prevent the rash and often unjust severities of inferior officers of the militia and yeomanry. He issued a positive order against the infliction of punishment, under any pretence whatever, not authorised by the order of a general officer in pursuance of the sentence of a general court-martial.* Any one who takes the trouble to look into the Cornwallis correspondence, will see by how ferocious a spirit the dominant class were animated in their determination to subdue the hostile population, and how shocked Lord Cornwallis, himself a soldier, was by this sanguinary disposition. He writes to Lord Portland †—

"It shall be one of my very first objects to soften the

* Cornwallis, "Correspondence," vol. ii., p. 355.
† Ib., vol. ii., p. 357.

ferocity of our troops, which I am afraid, in the Irish corps at least, is not confined to the private soldiers."

The militia he describes as " ferocious and cruel in the extreme when any poor wretches, either with or without arms, come within their power." Even when the rebellion was all but suppressed, we find him writing—

" The feeble outrages, burnings, and murders, which are still committed by the rebels, serve to keep up the sanguinary disposition on our side. . . The conversation of the principal persons of the country all tends to encourage this system of blood, and the conversation, even at my table, where you will suppose I do all I can to prevent it, always turns on hanging, shooting, burning, &c. &c.; and if a priest has been put to death, the greatest joy is expressed by the whole company." *

The Irish Act of 1798 had authorised the Lord-Lieutenant to constitute the courts-martial to be appointed under it as he thought proper, and of such persons as he pleased. The experience of what had taken place under this system led the British Parliament, when they passed the Act of 1803, to regulate the number of the members, and to limit the selection of members to officers of the King's forces, the militia, and the yeomanry. The recorded experience of Lord Cornwallis of the exercise of martial authority by the two latter probably induced Parliament, when thirty years afterwards it passed the Act of the 3rd and 4th William IV., to provide that officers of his Majesty's army should alone sit on courts-martial to administer martial law under that Act, and, by the regulations it imposed, to secure, prac-

* Cornwallis, " Correspondence," vol. ii., p. 371.

tically, as we have seen, that the courts-martial to try civilians should be subject to all the rules and conditions which insure justice being done to the soldier. I cannot but think that the abuse of martial law has been one of the main causes through which it has acquired the character for lawless and irresponsible power which has been ascribed to it in modern times.

But it is said that, as the necessity of suppressing rebellion is what justifies the exercise of martial law, and as, to this end, the example of immediate punishment is essential, the exhibition of martial law in its most summary and terrible form is indispensable. If by this it is meant that examples are to be made without taking the necessary means to discriminate between guilt and innocence, and that, in order to inspire terror, men are to be sacrificed whose guilt remains uncertain, I can only say I trust no court of justice will ever entertain so fearful and odious a doctrine. There are considerations more important even than the shortening the temporary duration of an insurrection. Among them are the eternal and immutable principles of justice, principles which never can be violated without lasting detriment to the true interests and well-being of a civilised community.

But is there any such necessity as is alleged? Surely, if a rebellion is raging, men enough will be taken red-handed, as it is termed, of whose guilt the proofs are patent and at hand. Such cases will furnish ready victims enough, even though the trials should be conducted according to the procedure of ordinary military tribunals. Can there be any such necessity as to justify the trial of a case which rests on circumstantial evidence alone, in hot and unseemly haste, without giving the accused the proper opportunity

to prepare for his defence, or upon evidence which
no properly organised military tribunal could properly
receive? The best and the most practical answer
is to be found in the fact that the 3rd and 4th
William IV., c. 4, provided, for the administration
of martial law under it, tribunals constituted practically like ordinary courts-martial, and insured that
the procedure to be adopted should be the same as
that used by these courts, or, if anything, still more
favourable to the accused.*

A question immediately connected with this branch
of the inquiry here presents itself, from the answer
to which a solution of the difficulty may possibly be
obtained. How are courts-martial of this description
to be constituted? Is it in the power of the authority
putting martial law in force to set aside the rules
which regulate the constitution of military tribunals,
both as to the number of members and the rank of
officers required, and to select his judges from any
class of persons he may choose? To put a strong case—
for though strong cases may sound absurd, and generally
are very unlikely to happen, they serve to illustrate
an argument and to test the truth of a proposition—
could a Governor take the first man he met in the
street, and set him to work to try reputed rebels for
their lives? I know not what may have been done
amid the irregularities which have attended the exercise
of martial law, in the way of employing civilians to

* It is a fact worthy of attention that when martial law was put
in force in Ceylon, in 1848, the proceedings on the various courts-
martial then held were all conducted, and the courts constituted,
according to the usual system of courts-martial in the army.
(See evidence of Sir T. H. Maddock before Ceylon Committee,
Qn. 3,981.—A. E. C.

sit on courts-martial, but in my opinion no civilian ought ever to be appointed a member of such a court. The term court-martial has from the time such a court was first known meant a military court, administering military law. The soldier must be taken to be acquainted with that law, for it is the law by which he is governed; but the civilian knows nothing of it, and ought to have nothing to do with it. The Act of William IV. took care that he should not. But if these courts-martial are to be, as I think they ought to be, composed of the officers of her Majesty's forces, *salvi sumus*, the difficulty is at end. For, no officer of the army can, according to the 152nd section of the Articles of War, sit on a court-martial without taking an oath to " administer justice according to the Articles of War and the Mutiny Act; and if any doubt shall arise which is not explained by the said Articles or Act, then according to his conscience and the best of his understanding, and the custom of war in the like cases." Now this oath derives a precise and intelligible meaning from the established course of procedure which has for two centuries prevailed in trials by courts-martial, and binds the officer who takes it to abide by that procedure. That oath cannot mean one thing to-day and another thing to-morrow. It cannot have one signification when an officer is sitting on a court-martial to try a soldier, another when he is sitting to try a civilian. It must mean, in either case, that the party taking the oath will deal with the subject-matter of the charge according to the Articles of War, as restricted and qualified by the Mutiny Act, and try the accused according to the established course of procedure. By imposing the obligation to take that oath, the Sovereign, who, subject to the restrictions of the Mutiny Act, is supreme in all matters connected with martial law, must be taken to have willed that wherever martial law is administered by officers in the service, it shall be administered according to the rules of that military procedure which by long experience has been found adapted to the ascertaining of truth and the protection of the accused. This question is not only one of general importance, but, as we shall see hereafter, has an important bearing on this particular case.

Gentlemen, I have now gone through what I have thought it necessary to say to you upon the subject of the power to exercise martial law, and as to the limitations under which it ought to be exercised, if it is capable of being put in force at all. I pass now to another branch of the inquiry, and that is, whether George William Gordon, who was put to death under the sentence of this court-martial, was amenable to its jurisdiction, if that jurisdiction existed.

I pointed out to you some time ago that when the Governor declared martial law in the county of Surrey, he excepted from its operation the town of Kingston, which is situate in and forms part of that county. It appears that Mr. Gordon usually resided a short distance from the town of Kingston. He had a place of business there, at which he was in the habit of attending. It appears that after this outbreak he was in Kingston on a visit. As I before told you, warrants having been issued for his apprehension, he went to the General's house to give himself up. He was arrested by the Governor and the Custos of the parish, Dr. Bowerbank, and he was by them taken on board a war steamer and conveyed to Morant Bay. Now, Kingston was not within the ambit of the martial jurisdiction, and the first question that presents itself upon this branch of the case—and a most painful question it is—is, whether this proceeding on the part of the Governor and the Custos was one which was justifiable or not. So far as I can gather, the Governor of Jamaica has no power to arrest. I do not know anything of the law of Jamaica of my own knowledge, but I gather this from the evidence given before the West-India Royal Commission, which I think sat in the year 1827 or 1828, both by the Chief Justice and the Attorney-General of the island. The whole course of the judicature of the island being then gone through, a question was put in the course of the inquiry whether the Governor had power to arrest criminals, and both those legal authorities said that he had not. I assume, therefore, that the Governor would not have authority, as Governor, to arrest Mr. Gordon. The Custos, being the principal magistrate of the parish, would, if he had any evidence before him, have authority as a magistrate to arrest or cause the arrest to be made. The law with regard to the power of a magistrate to arrest an offender, or a person presumed to be an offender, is thus correctly stated in the first volume of Burns' Justice, page 272:—" If the magistrate was not present when a crime has been committed, he ought not, at his mere discretion, to send a party accused to prison, but upon due consideration of the evidence adduced before him; and it was observed by Chief Justice Pratt, in the King v. Walker, 2 Wilson, 158, that in case a magistrate has

notice or a particular knowledge that a person has
been guilty of an offence, yet it is not sufficient ground
for him to commit the criminal, but in that case he is
rather a witness than a magistrate, and ought to make
oath of the fact before some other magistrate, who
should thereupon act the official part by granting a
warrant to apprehend the offender, it being more fit
that the accuser should appear as a witness than act
as a magistrate." I do not, however, think that this is
very material, because, in a case of high treason or
felony, any one of her Majesty's subjects may arrest
the supposed offender, subject always to this, that, if
it turns out that no offence has been committed, a
party so arresting another is liable civilly in damages
for an imprisonment which proves to have been un-
warranted. I am of opinion, therefore, that, in their
individual capacity, the Governor and the Custos, if
they had a really honest belief in the guilt of Mr.
Gordon, were warranted in apprehending him. But
for what purpose? In my judgment the only purpose
for which they could legitimately apprehend him was
in order to hand him over to the civil tribunals which
had power to take cognisance of the offence. The
power of the magistrate to arrest is a power derived
from the ordinary common law of the land. The
power of the peace officer or constable is the same.
The power or authority of any individual member of
the community to arrest a person who has been guilty
of a crime is in like manner derived from the ordinary
law. The duty which attaches upon the apprehension
of an offender under such circumstances is immediately
to hand him over to the first civil authority which can
be found—either to a peace officer or a magistrate, as

the case may be—in order that the party apprehended may be dealt with according to law—that is to say, according to the established law of the realm. These two gentlemen were not the ministers or apparitors of the martial authority. They had no power derived from the military authorities to take up this man for the purpose of handing him over to the martial law. Nevertheless, they did it. They did it by the exercise of the strong hand of power. Indeed, that has been avowed, and the motive of it has been avowed—namely, that it was thought that a conviction could not be got at Kingston; wherefore they took him from Kingston, where there was no martial law, and where he was safe, to Morant Bay, where there was martial law, and where a military tribunal could be formed to try and condemn him. Now, the question is whether this was an exercise of authority which invalidated what took place afterwards. I entertain a very strong opinion that the whole proceeding—the seizing him where he was, the putting him on board a steamer, and taking him to Morant Bay and handing him over to the martial tribunal—was altogether unlawful and unjustifiable. To Mr. Gordon it made the difference of life or death. I say so advisedly, because, after the most careful perusal of the evidence which was adduced against him, I come irresistibly to the conclusion that, if the man had been tried upon that evidence—I must correct myself—he could not have been tried upon that evidence—I was going too far, a great deal too far, in assuming that he could. He could not have been tried upon that evidence. No competent judge acquainted with the duties of his office could have received that evidence. Three-fourths—I had almost said nine-tenths—of the evidence upon which that man was convicted, and sentenced to death, was evidence which, according to no known rules—not only of ordinary law but of military law—according to no rules of right or justice, could possibly have been admitted; and it never would have been admitted if a competent judge had presided, or if there had been the advantage of a military officer of any experience in the practice of courts-martial, who knew by what rules a tribunal desirous of doing justice ought to be governed in the reception of evidence against a person who stands accused, especially of a man who stands accused upon a charge which involves his life. And I must further say that, looking at this evidence, I come irresistibly to the conclusion that no jury, however influenced by prejudice or passion, arising out of local or other circumstances, if they had been guided by a competent, impartial, and honest judge, could, upon evidence so morally and intrinsically worthless, and, as I shall show you presently, so wholly inconclusive as that evidence was, have condemned that man on the charges of which he was tried.

I know it has been said and written that it was justifiable to take Mr. Gordon to Morant Bay, because he had been as much guilty of high treason and sedition there as he had been at Kingston; and that as all crime is local, it was competent to the authorities to take or send him to be tried in that part of the island where he had been guilty of the offence laid to his charge. Now, it is perfectly true that crime is, in a legal sense, local, and that according to the law of England a man must be tried where the offence with which he is charged is alleged to have been committed. In our artificial division of the realm into counties, justice is administered with reference to these territorial divisions, and the man who is guilty of an offence in one county cannot, generally speaking, be tried in another. There are, indeed, exceptions to this rule. Some offences, from their very nature, may be said to be committed at the same time in more counties than one. If a man, intending to publish a libel, puts it into the post in London, with the intention that the libel shall be opened and read in another county, he may be charged and tried either where he commits the libel to the public means of communication and despatch, or in the county where it sees the light, and is, practically speaking, published. So in a case of conspiracy, if persons conspire to do an unlawful act, the conspiracy may be formed in county A, and some overt act in furtherance of it may be done in county B. In such case, the conspirators may be tried either in the county where the conspiracy was entered into and the plot or device hatched, or where it was carried into operation by the overt act. Again, by statutory enactment, in many instances a person may be tried in one of two counties. Take the common case of larceny. A man steals in the county of Middlesex, and he takes the stolen property into Surrey. He may be tried in either county. But it does not follow that, if a man is capable of being tried in one of two counties, and you have got him in a county where he may be tried, you can send him into another where he may also be tried, simply because you think you are more likely to get a conviction, or that justice is there going to be administered by a sterner judge, who will be likely to measure out a larger amount of punishment. That would be a most arbitrary and unwarrantable exercise of authority. If you have got the man where you can try him, you must try him there; and you have no right to take your choice of the tribunal because you think you may have a greater chance of success before the one than before the other. So that here, if Gordon could have been tried either at Kingston or in that part of the county of Surrey where martial law was in operation, having him at Kingston, they had no right to take him to Morant Bay to be tried. Now, I presume, he could have been tried at Kingston; for, so far as I have been able to gather, Kingston is the principal town of the county of Surrey. It has its assizes and its courts of law; justice is administered there, and it is the place at which justice ought to be administered for the county. There was nothing to prevent or interfere with the administration of justice at Kingston, or, indeed, so far as appears, anywhere else in the island.

Again, assuming that the offences with which Gordon was charged were committed in any other part of the county of Surrey, and not at Kingston, although in the artificial distinctions which we have between one county and another, and which no doubt prevail in the island of Jamaica, which has also been divided upon the model of England into counties, it is true you cannot try in one county an offence committed in another, we must not forget that Kingston is included in the county of Surrey, and that consequently an offence committed anywhere in the county of Surrey could be tried at Kingston. Therefore, that which has been plausibly put forward as a ground for transporting Mr. Gordon from Kingston to this other part of the county appears to me to be of no avail. But then the question whether the parties now accused are to be made responsible for the act of illegally bringing him within their jurisdiction, however unwarrantable, is a totally different thing. It is a very different question indeed when you come to deal with the parties who are now charged with murder upon this indictment. It is a very different thing to say that they are to be held responsible for what may have been an utterly illegal and unwarrantable act on the part of the Governor and the Custos in taking Mr. Gordon from Kingston to Morant Bay. When Mr. Gordon was brought within the ambit or sphere of the jurisdiction of martial law—assuming always, on this part of the case, that there was such a jurisdiction—it seems to me that it was not for the parties administering the martial law to inquire how he had been brought there. I will illustrate the matter by a case which has happened before now. Suppose a man to commit a crime in this country, say murder, and that before he can be apprehended he escapes into some country with which we have not an Extradition Treaty, so that we could not get him delivered up to us by the authorities, and suppose that an English police-officer were to pursue the male-factor, and finding him in some place where he could lay hands upon him, and from which he could easily reach the sea, got him on board a ship and brought him to England, and the man were to be taken in the first instance before a magistrate, the magistrate could not refuse to commit him. If he were brought here for trial, it would not be a plea to the jurisdiction of the court that he had escaped from justice, and that by some illegal means he had been brought back. It would be said, "Nay, you are here; you are charged with having committed a crime, and you must stand your trial. We leave you to settle with the party who may have done an illegal act in bringing you into this position; settle that with him." So here, although if Mr. Gordon had not been put to death, but had been subjected to some minor punishment, some of those scourgings or other things that we have heard of in Jamaica—if he had come to England and had brought an action for damages against Governor Eyre, it may well be that a jury of Englishmen, presided over by an English judge, would have awarded him exemplary damages for the wrong that had been done him; but that does not affect the question we are now considering, namely, whether, having been brought within the ambit of the martial law, he was liable to be tried under it. I cannot but think that he was. Another question, however, presents itself—namely, whether they had any jurisdiction over him in respect of any offence which he had committed against the martial law. The circumstances are very peculiar. It is true that, if Mr. Gordon was in a state of complicity with the parties who had broken out into this insurrection, it would be immaterial that no overt act had been done by him subsequent to the declaration of martial law. But if there was no evidence at all to warrant—and I think when you come to look at the evidence you will be of that opinion—if there was no evidence to warrant the allegation that he was an accomplice of the rebels—if all that could be alleged against him was that what he had previously said and

written had brought about the insurrectionary spirit,
which at last had broken out into open rebellion—if that
was all, then there was nothing which had been done
by Mr. Gordon that had not been done before martial
law was proclaimed; and a very grave question thereupon arises, whether he was amenable to martial law
at all. For, a man cannot commit an offence against
a law which law has no existence. If there is any
one principle which in the exposition and application
of the criminal law of this country is held more sacred
than another, it is that you cannot, by the *ex post
facto* application of a law, make a man liable to it for
an act done before the law came into existence. In
like manner, if that which is already an offence is by
Act of Parliament made a more serious crime, and
has a severer punishment attached to it, as where an
act which was before a misdemeanour is constituted
a felony, you cannot deal under the new law with
an offence committed before the law was altered.
If, indeed, the matter is one of procedure only, a
question of how a man shall be tried, this does not
fall within the rule; but no one, I imagine, would
seriously contend that the being subjected to such
a law as this so-called martial law, and being
tried before such a court-martial, was merely a matter
of procedure. Still, inasmuch as, if Mr. Gordon.
was the accomplice of those who had broken out into
rebellion, that would be a present offence, and as this
formed one of the charges against him, and was one of
the charges which the court-martial was directed to try,
I cannot say that, if they had any lawful jurisdiction,
this case was beyond it. But if the charge of complicity failed, and Mr. Gordon had done nothing for

which he was liable to be tried and punished since the
martial law was proclaimed, I have very great difficulty
in seeing how it is possible he should be amenable to
martial law for an offence, if it were an offence, committed before that law was called into existence,
and when it was no law at all. At the same time,
although I think that if the tribunal had been a
properly-constituted one, and the members of it
had understood what they were about, they would
have seen this difficulty, and have felt that they could
not convict Mr. Gordon, still I am very far from
saying that that would at all interfere with their jurisdiction to hear the case and decide it on its merits.
Possibly, but for that unfortunately intercepted letter,
in which a friend suggested to him the fitting line of
defence, but which this doomed and helpless man
was not allowed to see, the point might have been
brought to the attention of the tribunal; in which
case possibly, I dare not say probably, it might have
had the desired effect. But although this may be one
of the painful circumstances of this case, and may lead
us to lament the precipitancy with which this unfortunate man was hurried to his end, I do not think
that this is an objection which goes to the root of
the jurisdiction of the tribunal by which he was
condemned.

But here, Gentlemen, another difficulty presents
itself. Supposing that the true conclusion arising
from this discussion is that martial law is not the
wild, extravagant exercise of arbitrary and despotic
jurisdiction which has lately been represented—if
martial law is simply the military law applied to
civilians—then a very serious question arises. I allude

to the constitution of this tribunal. If, for the reasons I some time since pointed out to you, a court-martial to try a civilian under martial law must be constituted according to the military law, then this tribunal, which was composed of two officers of the navy and one officer of the army, was ill-constituted, and all its proceedings were null and void. For there is nothing in any of the Acts relating either to the military or the naval service—nothing in the Articles of War—nothing in the practice or usage of military tribunals which authorises the mixing of officers of the two services of the army and navy in the same court-martial. Officers of both services, when they sit on courts-martial, act under the authority of the Acts of Parliament and the Articles of War applicable to the respective services. In the army, a military court-martial must necessarily be composed of officers of the army; and it must consist of a certain number of officers. As to naval courts-martial, it is to be observed that no officer of the navy is warranted in holding or sitting on a naval court-martial unless by virtue of an order from an officer in the service holding a commission from the Admiralty to appoint courts-martial, which clearly was not the case in this instance. No court-martial can be held in the navy except upon the latter condition. Courts-martial on board ship, as analogous to regimental courts-martial, are things unknown and unauthorised in the service. A captain or commander of a ship, with the assistance of the first lieutenant, decides whether a man shall be subject to punishment or not; but if a court-martial is required by some graver case than usual, that court-martial can only be held by virtue of an order from an officer holding a commission from the Admiralty. Therefore, if this is to be treated as a naval court-martial there was no authority, because there was no such order to hold it. Besides, as I have said, there is no provision for the blending of the officers of the two services in the same court-martial. By the Mutiny Acts and the Articles of War, officers of the marines—who, you know, are soldiers serving at sea—may, for the purpose of holding courts-martial, be blended with the officers of a regiment of the line. So may officers of the artillery and other forces constituting the army of England. But there is no provision whatever, nor is the thing practically possible, that officers of the army and officers of the navy can be thus blended together. In either service the members of the court must take an oath, and by that oath they are sworn to act according to the Articles of War in the one case, and to the regulations of the Discipline Act of the navy in the other. The two laws are entirely different, and therefore the oaths which the officers belonging to the one service or the other are called upon by the laws of their respective services to take are not the same.

Again, with regard to tribunals of the one or the other service, as I said before, a certain number of officers are required. Courts-martial in the army are divided into general courts-martial, district courts-martial, and regimental courts-martial. Each must have its appropriate number of officers, nor can they act with less than the prescribed number. If this court-martial is to be considered as having been a military court-martial, it must be treated as a general court-martial, or as a district court-martial. In the first case, according to the 106th Article of War, being held in Jamaica, it should have consisted of not less than seven members, and two-thirds of the number must have concurred before sentence of death could be passed. If it is to be considered as having been a district court-martial, then by the 108th Article it should have consisted of at least five members, and by the 117th Article it had no power to award sentence of death at all. Therefore it appears to me that, supposing the military law, and not the martial law, in the sense in which that term is now used, is that which should have been acted on, then unquestionably this was not a properly constituted tribunal, and that would go to the very root of the whole jurisdiction.

And now this grave question presents itself: If there was no power in the Governor to put martial law in force, and consequently this court-martial was without authority, or if, by reason of any inherent vice in its constitution, it was without jurisdiction, and nevertheless proceeded to try and condemn Mr. Gordon, and cause him to be put to death, will his execution, under such circumstances, constitute the crime of wilful murder? As at present advised, what I shall lay down to you is this: when there is jurisdiction, but the jurisdiction is exercised under a misapprehension, either with reference to a person not within it, or in excess of the power of the tribunal, in such cases the persons acting with judicial authority would not be criminally responsible; but supposing that there is no jurisdiction at all, that the whole proceeding is *coram non judice*, that the judicial

functions are exercised by persons who have no
judicial authority or power, and a man's life is taken,
that is murder: for murder is putting a man to death
without a justification, or without any of those miti-
gating circumstances which reduce the crime of murder
to one of a lower degree. Thus in the case put by
Lord Coke of a lieutenant having a commission of
martial law, who puts a man to death by martial law
in time of peace, that, says Lord Coke, is murder.*

No doubt, where a jurisdiction of this kind has
been exercised under a mistaken belief in its existence, and a man has been put to death, although
legally this would be murder, no one would say
that it was so morally; and we cannot doubt that
in such a case the prerogative of the Crown, in
that which is said to be its brightest jewel and
ornament, the prerogative of mercy, would be exercised in the shape of pardon. But the law must

---

* Lord Hale writes as follows:—"If he that gives judgment of
death against a person hath no commission at all, if sentence of
death be commanded to be executed by such person, and it is
executed accordingly, it is murder in him that commands it to be
executed, for it was *coram non judice.* If a commission of the peace
issue, this extends not to treason, neither can justices of peace
hear and determine all treasons by force of this commission, for it
extends only to felonies (though some treasons are by Act of Parliament limited to their cognizance, as hath been before observed),
if they take an indictment of treason, and try and give judgment
upon the party, this is most certainly erroneous, and possibly
avoidable by plea; but I do not think it makes the justices guilty
of murder in commanding the execution of such sentence, for they
were not without some colour of proceeding therein, because all
treason is felony, though it be more, and the King may, if he
pleases, proceed against a traitor for felony; and antiently a pardon
of all felonies discharged some treasons (1 Ed. III., Charter of Pardon,

be vindicated; those who take upon themselves to exercise jurisdiction in exceptional cases, under the notion of some authority which forms no part or parcel of the common law of the land, must take heed what they do; and if, under the notion of a supposed jurisdiction, but which in fact does not exist, they take upon themselves to sit in judgment upon one of their fellow-men and put him to death, legally they are responsible upon a charge of murder. Therefore if you should be of opinion that this case is one in which the want of jurisdiction is either established, or is so far left a matter of question as that you think those who have exercised it ought to justify what they have done before a jury of their countrymen in an English court of justice, where every question will be carefully sifted and the law carefully ascertained and determined upon the most mature judicial deliberation, then I say, however sorry we may be that gentlemen who have intended to do their duty, and

---

13, 22, Assiz. 49, Co. P. C., p. 15), but it is a great misprision in such justices. The Justices of the Common Pleas cannot hold plea upon an indictment or appeal in capital causes; it will be at least erroneous, if not voidable by plea. But if they hold plea in appeal of death by writ, and give judgment therein for the party to be hanged, which is executed accordingly, I think it is an error, and a great misprision in them, but not felony, because they had colour to hold plea thereof by an original writ out of the chancery under the Great Seal. If in the time of peace a commission issue to exercise martial law, and such commissioners condemn any of the King's subjects (not being listed under the military power), this is without all question a great misprision and an erroneous proceeding, and accordingly adjudged in Parliament in the case of the Earl of Lancaster (Parl. 1 E. III., part 1, de quo supra, p. 344). And in that case the exercise of martial law in point of death in time of peace is declared murder (Co. P. C., p. 52).—A. E. C.

who believed themselves to have been acting under a valid authority, should be made amenable at the bar of a criminal court for the crime of murder, yet, if they have taken upon themselves to put a fellow-subject to death without lawful authority, they must be content to stand by the consequences of what they have done. If, in the exercise of an assumed power, they have, in putting this man to death, done that which the law will not justify them in doing, they must be amenable to the laws of their country.

I have now gone through the subject of the power to declare martial law, and of the jurisdiction of the accused in acting under it, and of the effect of the absence of such jurisdiction with reference to this charge of murder. I have felt deeply sensible of the exceeding difficulty of the task. I have been, for the most part, travelling over untrodden ground, with no beaten track to follow, and without the light of judicial decisions or of learned authority to guide me. I have not had the advantage of discussion at the bar, in which the knowledge, and research, and reasoning powers of learned and able men come to the assistance of the Judge. I have not had the benefit of judicial consultation. My colleagues have been absent on their respective circuits, and it was only yesterday that I was enabled to hold communication with the very learned and excellent Judge who sits by my side.* I have, however, done the best I could to put you in a position to discharge your duty in that part of this proceeding which falls within your peculiar province, which is to determine whether such a *primâ facie* case is made out for the prosecution as that the accused

* Baron Channell.

should be called upon to answer for their conduct before a jury of their country.

I now pass on to the second main branch of this inquiry—namely, whether, assuming that there was jurisdiction to try the deceased under martial law, that jurisdiction was honestly and *bonâ fide* exercised, or whether, as is suggested on the part of the prosecution, it was corruptly and *mala fide* exercised.

Supposing that the authorities were of opinion that Mr. Gordon was a mischievous and obnoxious character, of whom, for the peace and safety of the island, it was important to get rid, but as to whom there was not that amount of proof which would insure his condemnation before a regular tribunal, and that, with a view to his being unjustly condemned, they sent him into a district where martial law was being exercised, and supposing further that the tribunal before whom he was brought for trial entertained the same sinister purpose and determined to get rid of him, and although the evidence adduced against him was manifestly inconclusive, found him guilty, not upon the proof of the charge on which he was brought before them, but colourably and ostensibly upon that charge, and in reality because, for other reasons, it was deemed desirable to get rid of him; that would be a corrupt exercise of the judicial functions which that tribunal had to administer. A Judge who condemns a man on a charge on which his guilt is not proved, because he believes him to have been guilty of some other offence, or to be generally a man given to crime, is guilty of a gross abuse of his office, and if he were to put a man to death under such circumstances would, in my opinion, commit murder. But then such a charge is so serious, is one which so fearfully affects the character of all the parties alleged to have been concerned in so nefarious a conspiracy, that you would, doubtless, think it right to consider well whether there were facts to justify putting men upon their trial upon such a charge, nor would you do so except on what appeared to you sufficient grounds. At the same time, Gentlemen, it is one which I cannot withdraw from your consideration, and I must call your attention to the evidence which was given on the trial of Mr. Gordon, to the extraordinary character of that evidence, to the inconclusiveness of it, and to the conviction which took place notwithstanding the moral worthlessness of the proof. You must judge for yourselves as to whether you think that a case is made out on which the accused ought to be put upon their trial for having in their respective capacities dealt dishonestly and corruptly in the condemnation and execution of Gordon. If you think there is not, so far as this part of the case is concerned, you will throw out this indictment. If you think there is, you will find a true bill.

I am sincerely grieved, Gentlemen, to have to trouble you at such length; but I fear that with reference to this part of the case, I must trespass still further upon your time. I have before me the minutes of the proceedings on the trial of Gordon, and I must ask your attention to them. I have told you that the charges were these :—high treason against her Majesty Queen Victoria, and complicity with the parties who were engaged in the rebellion or insurrection at Morant Bay, on the 11th of October, 1865. The court having been duly sworn, the prisoner pleaded Not Guilty. Now comes the evidence. First you have a man of the name of John Anderson, a black, and a rebel, and himself liable to be tried. He gives this evidence :—

"The last time the prisoner went up to Stoney Gut he came to the chapel, Highland Castle, at Stoney Gut. He says to Paul Bogle—'They are going to hold a public meeting. We must get up some men for to go to Morant Bay to seek about the Backland, and if we don't get the Backland, all the buckra they will be die.' And after that Paul Bogle asked me if I would join them. I told him no I would not join it, because when all buckra died, how we going to manage, and he said if I do not join it they will shoot you. I was forced to travel away to Leathall Barracks. Paul Bogle got M'Laren to go up the mountain to look for hands, and to come to Morant Bay.

"Q. (By the Prisoner.) On what day did you see me at Stoney Gut?—A. Sunday.

"Q. In what month and what year?—A. This year, I know; June or July, I believe, but I did not date it down.

"Q. Was there any other person there besides Bogle and myself?—A. Plenty more.

"Q. Did I say that publicly in the presence of all?—A. Yes.

"Q. What time of day was it?—A. After chapel was over; about this time, 3 p.m.

"Q. You know me?—A. Yes."

Then a man of the name of James Gordon was called, and he said—

"Mr. Gordon sent all the people must gather up money, and send it to him, that he might pay it for the letter to go home to the Queen, and if the letter won't go, he will go himself to see the Queen face to face, and when we tell the man we not able to do that, if it is the Queen sent we will do so. And he said we must try, endeavour, and if we get the money we must send it in a letter, and send it to a post-office, and direct G. W. Gordon at the back, and he will receive it anywhere at all."

You observe that John Anderson and James Gordon were thus both examined *vivâ voce* in open court, and I think you will agree with me in saying that neither Anderson nor Gordon had said anything which could seriously affect Mr. Gordon on the charge of high treason, or complicity with those guilty of it. But observe what follows. John Anderson and James Gordon, having been implicated in the rebellion, had gone before a magistrate, when the accused was not present, and had made depositions against him, which depositions had been taken down in writing. Having been taken behind the back of the accused, they were clearly inadmissible. For if there is one rule more inflexible than another, it is that when you can call a living witness, you cannot make use of any deposition that he has made. He must come into open court, and state in the presence of the accused what he has to say against him. These two men were not only capable of being called, but had been called, and their evidence had fallen altogether short of what they had said behind the back of the accused; they had said little or nothing to affect him. Hereupon it occurs to the President to read their depositions as being more to the purpose, and their depositions were accordingly read. This is the deposition of John Anderson:—

"Paul Bogle asked me to join him, but not join the buckra. I know Mr. Espeut. I saw George Gordon go to Stoney Gut, and said he intend holding a meeting; that the blacks should kill all the whites. This was at Stoney Gut Chapel, Highland Castle, christened by G. W. Gordon, Paul Bogle, William Bogle, Wm. Buie. James Buie said if all the black would join him, he would take his stick and go to Morant Bay and make work.

"JOHN ANDERSON X his mark."

Next comes James Gordon's deposition :—

"Mr. G. W. Gordon sent up a letter to the Valley to say there will be a war"—not one word of that had he stated in the oral evidence—"and the whole of the people must be prepared for it. James M'Laren carried the letter up the Valley; and he also said that the people will get land free. I was sent up from St. David by Mr. Charles McLeon to give evidence."

I need hardly point out how much stronger the statement in the deposition is than what he had said just before in his oral testimony. These depositions, the witnesses being there present in court, could not properly be received; nevertheless they were read against the prisoner.

Now if ever there was a violation of the sound rules of evidence, it was the admission of these two documents (and the putting them in appears to have been the act of the president), the evidence having been given behind the back of the accused, and the witnesses having already been examined; and what makes it worse is that they were depositions made by men who may well have thought that by making these statements they would be likely to insure their own safety, they being known rebels. To use these depositions was one of the most lamentable departures from every principle of procedure that can well be imagined. To be sure, D. W. Mackenzie, justice of the peace, adds this postscript :—

"These men voluntarily came from St. David's, and were warned that the evidence must not be from fear, reward, or any promise, and were cautioned in the presence of all the prisoners not to state anything from fear."

What is meant by "all the prisoners" I know not. M.r Gordon, against whom the evidence was directed, certainly was not there. Then Gordon, one of these witnesses, is asked by the prisoner—

"How do you know the letter came from me?—*A*. Because it was signed George W. Gordon.

"*Q*. Do you know my signature?—*A*. No."

Then Gordon Ramsay, the Provost-Marshal, was called. This was a man who took a part in these unfortunate proceedings to which I would rather not further allude on the present occasion. He acted as prosecutor on the occasion of this trial. In an ordinary court-martial there ought to be a judge-advocate, an officer who is supposed to know something of the rules by which military tribunals are governed, and who acts as the adviser of the court. There appears to have been no such person upon this occasion, but Mr. Gordon Ramsay, who held the office of provost-marshal, that is, of executive officer of justice of the island, acted on this occasion as the assistant to the court. He was the prosecutor as well, and he pro- duced a deposition of one Thomas Johnson, made, as was alleged, upon his death-bed, the man having since died. This deposition was clearly inadmissible, as dying declarations are only admissible where the death of the deceased is the subject of the charge, and the cause of the death the subject of the dying declaration. It was, however, read, and was as follows:—

"*Morant Bay, October 17th,* 1865.—I, Thomas Johnson, now considering myself on my death-bed, but in my perfect senses, make this statement without fear or malice, trusting in God. I never attended a meeting, though asked by G. W. Gordon, of the parish of St. Thomas in the East, Member of Assembly. He twice asked me, but I would not agree, to throw up quatties and fippences as much as your hand can reach. I asked him why I do that for what Queen give me free already. He said, 'Who like for cat he eat, but by-and-by what that quattie and fippence will come to I must do it. He sent the money home. I said all the outside land we can get for nothing. Gordon said every man must give him 10s. a year, so that when taxes come in he can pay for taxes. Gordon had two meetings. Our houses are near. I mean his chapel is near my house. He sent a ticket to all the people to meet on certain hours, for what he had to tell them he would tell them. I did not go, but I heard what was said. 'People will the ticket keep.' That was Friday meeting; no prayers. Second meeting, prayers. My wife came from it. She told me I was not to go to Baptist meeting; they have no good for tell me. I must go to Mr. Panton, Port Morant. My wife said, also, Mr. Gordon told her, 'White man keep all the money, and make the people work for nothing.' I was in Mr. Grant's, the saddler's shop, when the Court-house was burnt. Mr. Grant said, 'I must be shut up with another boy.' When Mr. Grant heard the beating outside, Mr. Grant was attending to me the whole night, and gave me water. Mr. Gordon's people make disturbance, and Mr. Gordon teach them. All is Gordon's friends at Stoney Gut to do it."

Judge for yourself what such a piece of evidence is worth. Then a question is put by the court, "Did the dying man say that they were Mr. Gordon's friends at Stoney Gut, or did he mean to say he heard they were? A. He said "Gordon's friends; Gordon teach them." This question was put to this Mr. Ramsay, the Provost-Marshal, who was asked whether the dying man said one thing or meant another, certainly an extraordinary question. Then comes another deposition, a deposition made by two persons of the name of Peart and Humber, made in like manner before a magistrate, behind the back of the accused, these persons being living. They were in the island, and might have been examined before this tribunal, except, to be sure, that that would have involved the delay of a few hours, and it was deemed necessary, I suppose, to hurry on the trial in this way, in order to make an example of Mr. Gordon at the earliest moment. The trial took place so rapidly after his landing at Morant Bay that I suppose it might have been difficult to get these witnesses; but I cannot accept that as a reason why ordinary and most essential rules should be departed from.

"Personally appeared before me, one of Her Majesty's justices of the peace for the parish of Vere, William Robinson Peart and James Fyfe Humber, who, being duly sworn, maketh oath and saith: That on the 4th day of September they were present at the meeting held at the 'Alley,' when George William Gordon addressed the people in the following inflammatory language: 'My friends—I am here to-day to discuss the merits of Doctor Underhill's letter. We applied to the Custos for the use of the Court-house, but he refused, saying that no magistrate or vestryman signed the application. We petitioned the Governor—he is a bad man, my friends. What did he do, but sent over the petition to the Attorney-General for his advice, who, I firmly believe, my dear friends, is not sound; and he gave it as his opinion that the Custos did right to refuse the Court-house, and had it in his power to do so. Let me inform you that the magistrates and vestrymen are your trustees for the Court-house. Who elects the vestrymen? (A voice, "The planters.") It is your right and privilege; you pay taxes, and your money purchases the Court-house. The Governor is a bad man; he sanctions everything done by the higher class to the oppression of the poor negroes. Now, my friends, a few words as to the rate of wages and how you are treated by your employers. The moneys that is said to go for the cultivation of the properties goes in other ways that you ought to perceive. My people get 9s. per week: what do you get? (Several voices,

"2s. 6d., 1s., and 9d. per week; sometimes none at all.") (Mr. G.)—What is the price of rice at the Alley? (A voice, "7½d. for seven gills.") (Mr. G.)—In England it is a penny halfpenny to twopence per quart, showing that the peasantry in England are better off than those of Jamaica. Look at your clothes; half of you are naked. Your children and yourselves can't go to church for want of clothes. This is a serious question. The people of this parish ought to be paid £12 per year. The coolies get rich, because they get work continually; but you do not. (A voice, "The planters, after the bargains, crush us down, and give us one-half.") (Mr. G).—They report to the Queen that you are thieves. The notice that is said to be the Queen's advice is all trash; it is no advice of the Queen at all. I am glad to say that there are a few men in Vere who are loyal and serve their God. The people in Vere are in a very low state, and very much oppressed. Educate your children, and in time they will be able to take the leading parts in their country. Mr. Price and a few others that I could name are worthy men. These gentlemen love their people, but the gentlemen in Vere won't speak to you. I have been told by a great many of you that the planters work on Sundays, distilling rum. Why, you are putting fire to your own souls! Others of you who stickle at the price offered are ordered to leave the property. Sabbath-breaking is bringing down the curse of Heaven on Vere. What is to become of you as a people, and what is to become of your children? I will write to the Secretary of State and Lord 'Brougham' that I had been in Vere, and state the distress of the people. I was told by some of you that your overseer said, that if any of you attended this meeting he would tear down your houses. Tell him that I, George William Gordon, say they darn't do it. It is tyranny. You must do what 'Hayti' does. You have a bad name now, but you will have a worse then.'"

As to all this, it is really idle to say that it has any real colour of rebellion or treason in it. The man is declaiming before this black population, and descanting upon their alleged wrongs and grievances, calling this one and that one in office bad names. If agitation cf this description were to constitute high treason, there are a good many persons who would have to answer in a very serious way for what is with them pretty well every-day language. It is absurd to give to such language the colour and complexion of treason. To be sure the deposition makes Gordon say, "You must do what Hayti does." But, to say nothing of this evidence having been wholly inadmissible, who could believe that by these words Gordon meant to excite his hearers to treason and rebellion? Even supposing these witnesses intended to speak the truth, how far can this expression, "You must do what Hayti does," be relied upon, without our being perfectly satisfied that we have all the context to it, and have it in the precise terms in which the language was spoken? If the man had said, "One of these days, if oppression is carried to the uttermost, it may be a question of whether you may not have to do as they did at Hayti," such an expression would have been a very injudicious and very improper observation to have made; yet it would obviously not have been intended to provoke insurrection. Every one knows how easily the effect of language may be distorted. No disturbance did in point of fact take place after that meeting. But the observation to be made here is that this evidence was, from beginning to end, *in toto* inadmissible. No man in troubled times would be safe, if the reception of such testimony as this could be tolerated.

Next we have a letter from Mr. Gordon to a Mr. Chisholm, of the 11th of September, 1865 :—

" DEAR CHISHOLM,—I hope you are well. I have much

to say to you, but I shall not write, hoping to see you in a few days hence, when I go up to pay taxes. Please to tell Messrs. McIntosh, Clarke, and Boyle to inquire at P.O. for papers. I have been in Vere, where the poor people are very wretched, and positively starving. I never saw anything so bad. We need pray to God for help and deliverance. Remember me to all friends. I have been so busy that you must excuse haste."

There is certainly nothing in that letter that in the slightest degree savours of treason. It is the letter of a man who, having had actual inspection, describes the state of a portion of the population in strong terms. Then we get another deposition, as inadmissible as the last, and for the same reason. It appears to have been taken before a magistrate, Mr. Henry J. Bicknell, and is the deposition of Charles Chevannes. He says—

"Shortly after the first trial of the action Gordon v. Kettelhodt, I met Mr. George Wm. Gordon, and expressed to him my regret at his defeat. He said, 'Never mind; I hope yet to get my revenge; and if I don't get it my people will.'"

As to what that hoped-for revenge was—whether it was that he should bring another action against this Baron Kettelhodt, with whom he had got into a state of perpetual conflict, and hoped to defeat him, or whether he had any mischievous notion in his mind at the time he said this, or whether it was only the vapouring of a man who was seeking to hide the mortification of recent defeat, is a matter which it is impossible upon this evidence to determine. We then get another deposition of one George Thomas, residing at York, in the parish of St. Thomas-in-the-East :—

"These three weeks .they began on it. Paul Bogle and Moses Bogle have sent to call me and several others. When I went they swore me, and told me the appointed day. I would see what was done. The day appointed was Wednesday, the 11th of October, 1865. They (Paul Bogle and Moses Bogle) told me I was entitled to 4s. a day, and I never got it. Mr. Gordon never came there, but Mr. Bogle got his, Mr. Gordon's, handwriting, and he, Mr. Gordon, was the person who told Mr. Bogle the land was going to be free, and he, Mr. Gordon, put up Mr. Bogle to do all this rebellion. Paul and Moses Bogle said to me, that if I did not swear they would kill me. Tuesday night last, the 10th October, 1865, was the last meeting we had. I heard them say they were not to trouble Mr. Georges, because he is a friend of Mr. Gordon. I repeat that Mr. G. W. Gordon is the head of the rebellion. He put up the Bogles to do .it. I heard Paul Bogle say, on Wednesday, the 11th October, 1865, on the Parade, 'Good God! we can't get no fire. Look at the white men killing all the black people.' He, Paul Bogle, called for the fire. I have heard Mr. G. W. Gordon advising the people not to pay for their lands, and they must seek for the white people first. Monday, the 9th October, 1865, four policemen came to Paul Bogle yard, namely, William Fuller, Lake, and the other a Maroon young man, and McKay, with two constables. I know one of the constables' name to be Liston Davis, and the other to be Betty. I have seen at the meetings at Church Corner, James Dacres, Thomas Bogle, and the other Bogle that works Dr. Marshalleck's logwood dray. McLaren, of Church Corner, and a man named Grant, at Stanton Land, use to write at the meetings, and I have seen a small man from town. I hear he is a family to George Clarke at Paul Bogle house, and he all times write at Paul Bogle's. George Clarke and his father-in-law, Paul Bogle, get out, and he, Clarke, has nothing to do with this row. I have never seen him at the meetings."

This deposition, again, was wholly inadmissible, for the reason I have before given. It must have been mainly on the statement of this man, I suppose, that they came to the conclusion of Gordon's guilt. This man says that Gordon put Bogle to do this rebellion, and that it was all Gordon's doing, without in any degree or in any manner explaining upon what grounds he felt himself warranted in making that statement. I need not tell you that if, in the administration of justice, a man were to come into court as a witness, and say that a man was guilty of such and such an offence, that alone would not do. He must state facts and circumstances from which a court and jury may see that the assertion he makes is a well-founded one. Here the witness is stating, not facts, but merely his own conclusions. The evidence is not only inad. missible, but utterly worthless and inconclusive.

Then there is a paper of Mr. Gordon's, found in his portmanteau, put in, which is as follows:—"Public meeting. A public meeting will be held at ———, on the ——— day of ———, for the purpose of ———. The chair to be taken at ——— o'clock by ———." A valuable piece of evidence, certainly! Then a Mrs. Elizabeth Jane Gough was called, the postmistress at Morant Bay, and she says—

"There was a correspondence between Mr. Gordon and certain parties, George McIntosh, William Grant, the saddler, Wm. Chisholm, Jas. McLaren. I have seen a letter to Paul Bogle from the prisoner.

"*By the Court.* You can swear to the handwriting?—*A.* Yes; I know his handwriting well.

"*Q.* Look at that, and tell me if you know it?—*A.* That came in two packages; one to Chisholm and one to Paul Bogle, addressed by Mr. Gordon, in his writing I'll swear."

Here was shown a placard headed "State of the Island."

"*Q.* Are those in Gordon's handwriting?—*A.* They are.

"*Q.* Was it not customary for the prisoner to attend all vestry meetings?—*A.* Yes."

Now observe this question, I cannot help calling it an insidious one :—

" *Q.* And was it not an exceptional instance, his missing the very day of the slaughter?—*A.* It was; everybody thought it very strange."

In the first place, the question put as to its being an exceptional instance was a very marked one; in the next, that the witness should be allowed to say that everybody thought it very strange was clearly wrong.

" *Q.* Have you seen or heard of the meetings here?—*A.* I never heard of them.

" *Q.* Were they kept secret?—*A.* I don't know.

" *Q.* (*By the Prisoner.*) Are you aware that I have been corresponding for years with Bogle?—*A.* I only remember one letter about some sugar.

" *Q.* When was my last letter to Bogle?—*A.* Can't say.

" *Q.* Was it more or less than two months?—*A.* I cannot remember the exact time.

" *Q.* Are you not aware that Chisholm is an old servant of mine, and that I have always been in correspondence with him more or less?—*A.* I was not aware he was ever a servant of yours.

" *Q.* Then I will make it 'friend'?—*A.* When prisoner comes late in the Bay, he always says he will get his glass from Chisholm; that is all I know.

" *Q.* Did a letter come through the post for McIntosh lately?—*A.* There was a paper with a penny stamp on it for McIntosh.

" *Q.* What induced you to take that placard out of the cover or wrapper?—*A.* It was a habit at the post-office to take out papers, read them, and return them.

" *Q.* When the seal was off, or how did you get it out?—*A.* A book-post parcel with the ends clear.

" *Q.* Did you know I was suffering from indisposition?—*A.* I never heard."

The following document, seized at the post-office at Morant Bay, October 11, 1865, but which in fact had been issued prior to a meeting which took place two months previously, was then read:—

"STATE OF THE ISLAND.

" A requisition, numerously signed for a public meeting, to consider 'the condition of the people,' having been presented to the Custos of St. Thomas ye East, his honour has, we learn, appointed the meeting for that purpose at Morant Bay. We trust that there will be a good meeting, and that the people will not on that day allow themselves to be interfered with by any of those who have already written to their disparagement, and made statements without proper foundation, which have so misled her Majesty's Government as to cause the very indiscreet despatch which the Right Hon. Mr. Cardwell, Secretary of State, was induced to send to Mr. Eyre, in reply to the St. Ann's memorial. This document ought to be well handled in a loyal spirit. We know that our beloved Queen is too noble-hearted to say anything unkind, even to her most humble subjects, and we believe that Mr. Cardwell and her Majesty's ministers are gentlemen too honourable and honest in their intentions wilfully to wound the feelings of her Majesty's Colonial subjects. But we fear they have been deceived and misled, and the consequence is a serious grievance to our people; but we advise them to be prudent, yet firm, in their remonstrances, and we have no doubt that ' truth' will ultimately prevail.

"People of St. Ann's,
Poor people of St. Ann's,
Starving people of St. Ann's,
Naked people of St. Ann's,

"You who have no sugar estates to work on, nor can find other employment, we call on you to come forth, even if you be naked, come forth and protest against the unjust representations made against you by Mr. Governor Eyre and his band of Custodes. You don't require Custodes to tell your woes, but you want men free of Government influence; you want honest men, you want men with a sense of right and wrong and who can appreciate you. Call on your ministers to reveal your true condition, and then call on Heaven to witness and have mercy.

"People of St. Thomas ye East, you have been ground down too long already. Shake off your sloth, and speak like honourable and free men at your meeting. Let not a crafty, jesuitical priesthood deceive you. Prepare for your duty. Remember the destitution in the midst of your families, and your forlorn condition. The Government have taxed you to defend your own rights against the enormities of an unscrupulous and oppressive foreigner, Mr. Custos Ketelhodt. You feel this: it is no wonder you do. You have been dared in this provoking act, and it is sufficient to extinguish your long patience. This is not the time when such deeds should be perpetrated; but as they have been, it is your duty to speak out, and to act too! We advise you to be up and doing, and to maintain your cause; you must be united in your efforts. The causes of your distress are many, and now is your time to review them. Your Custos, we learn, read at the last vestry the despatch from Mr. Cardwell, which he seemed to think should quiet you; but how can men with a sense of wrong in their bosoms be content to be quiet under such a reproachful despatch?

"Remember that 'he only is free whom the truth makes free.' You are no longer slaves, but free men. Then, as free men, act your part at the meeting. If the conduct of the Custos, in wishing the despatch to silence you, be not an act of imprudence, it certainly is an attempt to stifle your free expression of opinions. Will you suffer this? Are you so short-sighted that you cannot discern the occult designs of Mr. Custos Ketelhodt? Do you see how, at every vestry, he puts off the cause of the poor until the board breaks up, and nothing is done for them? Do you remember how he has kept the small-pox money, and otherwise mis-distributed it, so that many of the people died in want and misery, while he withheld the relief; how that he gave the money to his own friends, and kept it himself, instead of distributing it to the doctors and ministers of religion for the poor? Do you perceive how he shields Messrs. Herschel and Cooke in all their improper acts? You do know how *deaf* he is on some occasions, and how *quick of hearing* on others. Do you remember his attempting tyrannical proceedings at the elections? But can you and the inhabitants of St. Thomas ye East longer bear to be afflicted by this enemy to your peace—a Custos whose feelings are foreign to yours? Do your duty at the meeting to be held. Try to help yourselves, and Heaven will help you.

"More anon."

This was a placard published some time before, in anticipation of a general meeting at this place. That meeting, probably, was the one at which he made the speech spoken to by the two witnesses. At all events, when the meeting took place no mischievous consequences whatever arose out of it. And a man must have a very acute power of detection who can find in this placard anything more than the language of an agitator and a demagogue, who, while seeking to stir up strife and to keep up excitement in the minds of those whom he addresses, may be as far as possible from any intention of actual rebellion or insurrection.

Then a man of the name of McLaren is called. He was called in after he had been condemned to be hanged. He had been tried and sentenced. I may say, therefore, without using the term figuratively, that he came in with a rope round his neck. He says—

"I knew Mr. Gordon was a member of the House of Assembly.

"Q. (*By the Court.*) Do you know Mr. Gordon has something to do with the rebellion?—*A.* That I don't know of.

" *Q.* Did you ever hear of Mr. Gordon being connected with Paul Bogle?—*A.* Paul Bogle always voted for him.

" *Q.* Do you know James Gordon?—*A.* I know several James Gordons.

" *Q.* (*By the Prisoner.*) Did I ever send you up the mountain to raise money, or in any way tell the people not to pay for land, or anything improper?—*A.* No."

Well, nothing was elicited from this man, who was hanged shortly afterwards. Ramsay then produced another letter from the prisoner to one E. Smith, marked private. It was written after the outbreak had occurred. I think this is a letter of very great importance. It was admitted by the prisoner to be in his handwriting, and it was as follows :—

" MY DEAR SIR,—I thank you for yours of the 12th, only just to hand, and shall attend to the two cheques; but since yesterday the door to money transactions seems closed, and will, I fear, get worse till some order be restored. I lament deeply the report that my good friend Mr. Hire is amongst the slain. What a sad, sad work, superinduced by the arbitrary conduct of the poor Baron! What an appointment for the Governor to have made, and what a result! I truly deplore all that has occurred. I always advised peace and patience to the fullest extent; but I fear the sending away of Jackson, and the conduct of the C. P. and Justice, caused the people to lose all confidence and hope in anything like justice. In my opinion, this is the true cause of immediate discontent, and how easily could it have been avoided! I feel much for many who have suffered in this sad scene.

" Believe me, yours faithfully,

"E. C. Smith, Esq. " GEORGE W. GORDON.

" I am weak and unwell."

Mr. Hire was one of the persons who had been unhappily killed. This letter of Gordon's is a letter to a private friend. Gordon could not have anticipated

K

that it would be intercepted, and it may be fairly taken as representing his genuine sentiment. That letter having been read, another is put in—

"19*th June*, 1865.

"DEAR CHISHOLM,—I shall be up, D.V., by the end of this week, and hope to find all right. See inclosed. We must not lose heart, but persevere in the good. Best wishes.

"Yours very truly,
"GEORGE W. GORDON."

Then, although Mrs. Gough had been already examined, a deposition of hers is put in :—

"Elizabeth Jane Gough, widow, now staying in the city of Kingston, being sworn, saith—

"I am post-mistress at Morant Bay. For some time past, since the appearance of Dr. Underhill's letter, Mr. George William Gordon has been carrying on a regular correspondence through my post-office with George Mackintosh, William Chisholm, and William Grant, and James McLaren. He wrote McLaren about two posts, I think, before the breaking out last Wednesday at Morant Bay. I have also seen letters pass through the post-office from him to Paul Bogle, but not very often. The bag that arrived on Thursday night after the murders has not been opened. This bag is in Kingston post-office not opened, so, I think, Mr. Brymer told me. The last one to James McLaren was very thick, not a single letter. From McLaren's last words I think there must have been letters in it for other persons. I have received a packet of printed papers, addressed in Mr. Gordon's handwriting to Paul Bogle, and another to William Chisholm. They came by the same post, shortly after the publication of the Queen's advice. Paul Bogle has always been sending for letters, though he did not say from whom he expected them. Mackintosh also, the post before the outbreak, was asking for letters, he did not say from whom. I have seen letters from him addressed to Mr. Gordon; those letters were posted by him, and being late he paid after to forward them. I read one of the printed papers out of the packet addressed Paul Bogle. I gave it to Mr. Richard Cooke. I had one in the post-office, Morant Bay, at the time of the outbreak. I had it in the Z. hole. The heading of it was 'To the people of St. Ann's and St. Thomas-in-the East.'"

That is the paper I have already read. She goes on:—

"It called on the people to be up and doing. It contradicted what was said in the Queen's advice; but I can't exactly tell you the words. It was not signed, but the wrappers on both packets to Bogle and Chisholm were in Mr. Gordon's handwriting. I know that Mr. Gordon and Bogle are intimate. Every one in that district knew this."

This, again, is a deposition, and was therefore clearly inadmissible. This was the whole of the evidence for the prosecution. Then one Testard, a shopkeeper, was called for the defence. The president having suggested that Mr. Gordon, who had been in the habit of attending the vestry meetings, had not attended the particular meeting at which this outbreak took place, and having pointedly put the question to a witness whether that was not a suspicious circumstance, it became important for Gordon to prove that it was illness that had prevented his attendance. I certainly should have thought that his being present at the meeting would have been a much stronger fact against him than the being absent. However, finding what was the impression on the president's mind, he naturally desired to show how he had been kept away, and he called this witness Testard, who is asked—

"Q. Did you call at Kingston and find me sick some two weeks ago?—A. I called for a Mr. Mesquita, and finding he was gone to Mr. Gordon's, I went there. I saw Mr. Gordon on the sofa, but I could not say if he was sick; he was dressed. Mr. Mesquita and I left together."*

Such was the trial of Mr. Gordon. This is the whole of the evidence upon which the deceased man was found guilty of high treason, sentenced to death, and executed. Setting aside the fact that, for the reasons I have given, according to all the rules of legal or military procedure, or according to the rules which ought to obtain in every procedure whatever, the great bulk of that evidence was inadmissible, you have to consider whether, the evidence having been admitted, it was such as that a tribunal, honestly discharging its duty, could find a man guilty upon it of a crime a conviction for which must be followed by his death; or whether, from its character and its utter inconclusiveness, you see any reason to think that the inquiry was entered on with a determination to condemn Mr. Gordon, upon any evidence, however insufficient, and to put him to death.

I think there cannot be the least doubt that an opinion was universally prevalent in the island that it was through Mr. Gordon's instrumentality, through his

---

* Mr. Gordon had first desired to call a Dr. Major, who he said could prove that the state of his health had prevented him from attending the vestry meeting at Morant Bay on the 11th of October. The provost-marshal having been sent from the court to look for the doctor, returned shortly afterwards, saying that "Dr. Major was not in the Bay." Hereupon the Commissioners observe, that "considering the importance then attached to Mr. Gordon's absence from the vestry on the 11th October, it would have been much more satisfactory if some delay had been allowed in order that Dr. Major might have been sent for to speak to the state of his health." In the view thus taken by the Commissioners it seems impossible not to concur.—A. E. C.

speeches and writings, and the systematic agitation he had for some time been keeping up, that the mutinous and rebellious spirit had been engendered which broke out at last into this unhappy insurrection. The negroes appear to have believed that they had serious causes of complaint. The old animosity, arising from the relation of master and slave, although that relation had ceased, had probably left, even in the minds of the posterity of those who suffered under the old system, a feeling of enmity towards the white men, and a jealousy of their superiority. Besides this, they thought they had grievances, which may have been imaginary, but which may have been more or less real. They complained that they could not get justice administered when disputes arose between them and the whites. They complained of a serious grievance in respect of what was called the "Backlands," lands to which they claimed a right, and from which it was sought to eject them.*

Now it may have been that Gordon was partly in-

---

* I understand that the dispute respecting the so-called "Backlands" arose under the following circumstances:—Land belonging to one or two estates running up into the mountains had been thrown out of cultivation, and, as it is called, suffered to run to bush, and the quit-rents due to the Crown had not been paid for a period of seven years. The negroes were told that if they paid these arrears of quit-rent, they might cultivate and enjoy the lands rent free. Trusting to this assurance, they paid the arrears of quit-rent and brought the land into cultivation. Some short time before the outbreak, Mr. Hire, the agent of the owner of the estate in question, asserted the right of the owner, who had not been a party to the representation made to the negroes, and sought, on behalf of the owner, to dispossess and eject the negroes, who, however, resisted and maintained possession by force. Hereupon legal proceedings were instituted against the blacks, which proceedings

fluenced by the belief that these negroes were suffering
under certain wrongs; he may have been partly influenced by a notion that he, too, had wrongs to
complain of at the hands of the authorities. He
had been dismissed from his office of justice of the
peace at the instance of Baron Ketelhodt, the Custos
of his parish. He had been put out of his office
of one of the churchwardens of the vestry of the
parish, again at the suggestion of the Baron, on
account of his having joined the Baptist persuasion.
He had brought an action against Baron Ketelhodt
in which he had been defeated, and he ascribed his
defeat to the influence of the authorities over the jury.
As a member of the Assembly, he had been in fierce
opposition to the Governor. Among the motives which
may have induced Mr. Gordon to keep up this system
of agitation may have been the hostility and conflict
into which he had got with the authorities, both with
the Governor and with the Custos, Baron Ketelhodt.
But, on the other hand, Mr. Gordon was a man of
too great intelligence to be deluded into the
belief that open violence and insurrection could be
attended with any beneficial results to the black population. As you see from the language he uses, he
was a man of considerable education, and must,
therefore, have been well aware that, however it
might gratify him to keep up this system of agitation, yet an actual rebellion could only lead to
the most calamitous disasters to the negroes. Whatever vapouring and idle language he may have

were pending when the outbreak took place. This is the motive
assigned for the murder of Mr. Hire, notwithstanding the latter
was known to be a friend of Gordon.—A. E. C.

indulged in, he could not have supposed that the
negroes, undisciplined, unorganised, unarmed, unpre-
pared, could stand against such forces as could speedily
be brought against them. He must have known that
even a temporary success must necessarily be followed
by the application of the force of this country to
subdue the rebellion, and that it could only end in
disaster to everybody concerned, probably to himself
among the foremost. I think it, therefore, next
to impossible that he contemplated the outbreak
which took place.

Possibly, in addition to the motives I have
already pointed out, like many an agitator who has
gone before him, he was incited by the gratification
which proceeds from the consciousness of power
arising from the exercise of dominion over the
minds of men, by the sense of self-importance which
results from occupying the attention of the public, by
the gratification which arises from the applause and
admiration of the multitude, and, while it suited his purpose to keep the passions of the black population in a
state of ferment, bordering upon outbreak, he per-
suaded himself that by the mastery he possessed over
them he could keep them under subjection and control.
In this, like many an agitator who has preceded him, he
was deceived. That this system of agitation, working
upon the minds of an ignorant, unenlightened population, capable of sudden outbreaks of passion, and
which it then becomes impossible to control, did
produce a state of excited feeling, which, when the
torch, so to speak, was applied to the train, exploded
in this terrible calamity, I think there cannot be the
shadow of a doubt. But so far from there being any

evidence to prove that Mr. Gordon intended this insurrection and rebellion, the evidence, as well as the probability of the case, appears to me to be exactly the other way. That letter of his, written to a private friend, and which he could not expect would be intercepted, and which I have no doubt was a genuine one, fully shows that his feeling on hearing of the outbreak was that of surprise and sorrow. Yet I can quite understand, considering all he had said and done, and that he had been the master spirit that had fostered and kept alive this discontented spirit among the negro population, that when the insurrection actually broke out, the authorities would be led to suppose that he was at the bottom of these lawless proceedings, and therefore thought it right to institute proceedings against him. It may have been that Colonel Nelson and the members of the court-martial, participating in the general belief in Mr. Gordon's guilt, may have suffered their minds to be unduly operated upon thereby to his prejudice, yet without any imputation on the honesty of their intention. On the other hand, it is possible that, thinking that Gordon was the cause of the calamity which had occurred, and that though there might not have been any intention on his part that there should be a rebellious outbreak, he was nevertheless so morally responsible for it that he ought to be brought to condign punishment, and that such an example would have the effect of at once annihilating the insurrectionary movement, and that his removal would be for the future peace of the island, they determined upon his destruction. He was a man who was in violent opposition to the authorities, and was in the habit of reviling them and calling their acts in question. He was a man who kept the minds of the negro population in a perpetual state of agitation by the power and influence that he exercised over them. He was a man, therefore, obnoxious to the government, and whom it might be thought desirable to get rid of if possible. It may be that, in furtherance of this purpose, the parties now accused enacted their respective parts in the condemnation and execution of the deceased. It is for you, gentlemen, to say what you think is the true solution of these proceedings, and of Mr. Gordon having been convicted upon such evidence as I have called your attention to. It is entirely a matter for the exercise of your judgment. I have, to the best of my ability, put before you the grounds upon which that judgment should be exercised. No doubt in the result a lamentable event has taken place. A man has been condemned, sentenced to death, and executed upon evidence which would not have been admitted before any properly constituted tribunal, and upon evidence which, if admitted, fell altogether short of establishing the crime with which he was charged. You must judge whether, looking at the whole train of circumstances from the time of his apprehension to the time of his conviction and execution, you think that what was done in condemning and putting this man to death was honestly done or not.

And here, with reference to the charge against Mr. Gordon, I must take the opportunity of observing that intention is at all times of the essence of crime. I have seen it written—and I confess I almost shuddered as I read it—that it was justifiable to send Mr. Gordon to a court-martial to be tried, because a court-martial would be justified in convicting a man when mischief had resulted from acts of his, although that mischief had been entirely beyond the scope of, or even contrary to, his intention; as if it could make any difference in the quality of the offence for which a man was tried, whether he was tried before one tribunal or another. If that was the principle upon which they proceeded in Mr. Gordon's case, I can only say that it was as lamentable a miscarriage of justice as the history of judicial tribunals can disclose. *

* In Mr. Finlason's recent treatise on martial law I find (p. 61) the following passages:—

"The real key to the subject of martial law as distinct from ordinary law is, that its scope is not so much legal culpability as military exigency, or, in other words, not so much criminality as public safety; and hence, although at common law the criminal *intent* is always so important, and, indeed, generally essential (always in capital crimes), it is not so in martial law, which looks rather at the actual than the intentional cause of the mischief, and the necessity for an exemplary penalty.

"The greatest authorities of the common law itself distinguish between the criminal intent, which is essential to the legal guilt, and that matter of fact, quite apart from actual intent or guilt, which may justify even a sentence of death under martial law in time of civil war or rebellion, and recognise that the nature and scope of martial law, as of war, is rather the suppression of hostility and the removal of danger, by means of terror, than the vindication of law.

"The great difference here arises, as has been already pointed out, from the distinction between the scope of common law and of martial law, in that the former mainly regards guilt, the latter chiefly regards danger. The one, therefore, exacts strict legal proof of guilt, and especially the intent; the other, looking rather to the danger, looks only to the actual cause of the danger, and less to the intent, and to the actual or probable result of the punishment to be inflicted on persons supposed to be implicated.

"In time of peace the court can afford to be strict, critical, and technical in the definition of offences or the proof of guilt;

Gentlemen, it may be that all I have said upon the subject of the law will have left you, as I own candidly it still leaves me, not having the advantage of judicial authority to guide me, nor of forensic argument and disputation to enlighten and instruct me, in some degree of doubt. Let me, therefore, add that if you are of opinion, upon the whole, that the jurisdiction to exercise martial law is not satisfactorily made out, and that it is a matter which ought to be submitted to further consideration on the trial of the accused before a competent court, where all the questions of law incident to the discussion and decision of the case may be fully raised and authoritatively and definitively considered and decided, I must say I think that the safer course will be to let this matter go forward. If there was a power to put martial law in force, and consequently jurisdiction to try persons under it, that will be safely ascertained and firmly established by judicial decision; if there was none, it follows that there has been a miscarriage of justice which calls for inquiry, and as to which further inquiry ought to take place. If, however, upon the review of the authorities to which I have called your attention, and of the enact-

but in times of great public danger there really is not time for it, and there would be no sense in it. The question is, who has caused the danger, or helped to cause it, and who are those whose prompt punishment will be most deterrent. At such a time, if it is plain that a man has caused a rebellion, and that his death will stop it, what does it matter whether he directed exactly what has happened?"

I cannot too strongly express my dissent from, or my thorough disapprobation of, this most dangerous and pernicious doctrine, for which I am glad to think there is no authority whatever. A passage cited from Lord Hale, if rightly understood, is manifestly nothing to the purpose.—A. E. C.

ments of the Jamaica statutes, and the recognition and reservation of the power of the Crown in the Acts of Parliament, you think the accused ought not further to be harassed by criminal proceedings, and that the case against them ought not to be submitted to the consideration of a jury, you will say so by ignoring this indictment; upon this you must exercise your own judgment. Again, on the second branch of the case, in which we take the legality of martial law for granted, if you think that although there may have been a mistake, and a most grievous mistake, in condemning and sending this man to death, yet that the proceedings were done honestly and faithfully, and in what was believed to be the due course of the administration of justice, again I say you ought not to harass the accused persons by sending them for trial to another tribunal. If, on the other hand, you think there is a case which, at all events, calls for further inquiry and for an answer on the part of those who stand charged with this most serious offence, then you will find a true bill.

Gentlemen, I have only one more word to say to you before I leave you to the discharge of your important functions. These sad events have occupied a large portion of the public attention, and few persons have not felt an interest in the ample discussion of them which has taken place. Persons have adopted different views, and taken different sides. To some it has appeared that, when it is borne in mind that this insurrection was crushed in a moment, that as soon as the soldiers made their appearance, few as they were in numbers, the black men fled, and the only business of the soldiers was to pursue and hunt

them up, and bring them in as rebels before the
martial tribunals, this prolonged martial law, and this
fearful amount of execution—these terrible scourgings
with instruments of torture hitherto unknown and un-
heard of—are things which have brought a reproach,
not only upon those who were parties to them, but
upon the very name of Englishmen. Others have
thought that, as this insurrection, if it had been permitted to run its course, and had not been crushed
in the outset, might have been attended with consequences of the most fearful character, anything that
could be done for its suppression and extinction—any
means—no matter what—no matter how extraordinary
—how contrary to every principle of law—were justifiable in order to achieve so desirable an end. Opposite and conflicting views are entertained upon this
question. Having entered so largely into these matters, I feel bound to say—for I should be sorry not to
do justice to an absent man—that, looking to the
general consternation and alarm which pervaded the
island—looking to the circumstances in which the
white population and the authorities of the country
were placed, with reference to the proportion, the
small proportion, which the white population bore
to the black, to the mere handful of military force
that there was, and to the consequences, too horrible
to think of, which might have ensued if this insurrection had not been suppressed, to the threat by the
insurgents of destroying the white men, and their
reported intentions as to the white women,* I think if

---

* In my charge to the Grand Jury I stated that the insurgents had
avowed an intention to spare the white women, and to "keep them
for themselves." My attention having been since invited to the

ever there were circumstances which, if it be lawful to put martial law in force, called for the application of it,

evidence on this point, I am bound to say that the proof on which this charge against the insurgents rests is but slight. It consists of the statement of four witnesses. The first was a Mrs. Herschell, who first made a deposition, and afterwards gave evidence before the Commissioners, wherein she stated that a single rebel, who called at her husband's house to demand a gun or pistol, was overheard by her to say to some of her people that they were going to take the lives of the white men, but were not going to hurt the ladies. By the time this reaches Governor Eyre it receives the significant addition, "but were going to reserve them for themselves," which makes all the difference. In another instance, a band of negroes attacked the residence of a Mr. Harrison, the manager of the Hortley Estate, declaring their intention of killing every white,- women and children included. Mr. Harrison contrived to evade pursuit, and he and the principal negro woman on the estate succeeded in hiding Mrs. Harrison and the other ladies and children in the canes. Foiled in their endeavour to discover them, one of the rebels called out, "Never mind the Buckra women; we can get them when we want." (Mr. Harrison's evidence, p. 46, Qn., 2,049; and Diana Blackwood, p. 535, Qn., 26,965, and *seq.*) It being clear from the evidence that the purpose of these insurgents was to put the women and children to death, the parting words of this rebel are certainly capable of a different construction from that which has been put on them. Diana Blackwood, the black woman in question, certainly adds, "We know not what to do with them." But this may have had reference to their not having been able to discover the women to kill them. It appears also from the statement of a Mrs. Hutchins, who was examined before the Commissioners, that on a mob attacking her house, and one of them being about to kill her, another of them said, "Don't kill her; you want a wife." But this may possibly have been said to save her life. Practically, however, except so far as the criminality of the insurgents is concerned, all this is of little importance, for had the negroes succeeded in destroying the male part of the white population, the situation of the white women, when left entirely at the mercy of the black men, would have been one which it is dreadful to contemplate. (Evidence, p. 42, Question 1,898, and see deposition, part i., p. 72.)

it was this case of the insurrection in Jamaica. Nor do I think that it is for this Court, with reference to this particular trial, which took place shortly after martial law was declared, to enter into the question of whether that law was kept up longer than it needed to have been.* All that it is necessary for us to consider to-day is whether there was any power to put martial law in force, and if so, whether in this particular instance it was honestly applied.

Gentlemen, I have referred to the conflicting views which have been taken of this question for this purpose alone:—All of you, or nearly all of you, may have formed opinions of your own upon this much agitated and debated question—whether those who exercised this martial law to the extent to which it was carried ought to be held up to public reprobation, and if possible brought to punishment; or whether, on the other hand, they ought to be crowned with the approval of a grateful country, as having faithfully discharged a difficult and arduous duty. Upon those two conflicting views you may have formed your own opinions; but for God's sake do not let them influence you to-day. Passion and prejudice should never, under any circumstances, be allowed to enter into the sanctuary of justice. Consider this case as though it stood alone—as though there were no question of executions and torture on the one hand, or of the necessity of suppressing the negro insurrection on the other. You have to ask yourselves what is the law so far as we are able to ascertain it, and then whether that law has been truthfully, faithfully, and honestly administered.

* See concluding note, *post.*

Gentlemen, I have detained you at very great length. I regret it exceedingly; but the importance, and gravity, and difficulty of the case is such that I felt I could not say a word less to you than I have said. I have done my duty to the best of my ability; you will now do yours according to what in your consciences you believe to be due to the justice of the case as between the accusers and the accused, between those who ask for justice at your hands, in respect of the bringing George William Gordon to an untimely end, and those against whom this indictment for wilful murder will be preferred before you for having been the authors of his death.

The Grand Jury having, on ignoring the indictment against Colonel Nelson and Lieutenant Brand, made a formal presentment, strongly recommending that martial law should be more clearly defined by legislative enactment, I am reluctant to take leave of the subject without adding the expression of my opinion to that of the Grand Jury that the subject of martial law should be settled by legislative interposition, or without also protesting, so far as in me lies, and with whatever of weight and authority belongs to the office I have the honour to hold, against the exercise of martial law in the form in which it has lately been put in force. Thrice in little more than half-a-century—to say nothing of the horrors perpetrated in putting down the insurrection in Jamaica in 1760—in Ireland, in Demerara, in Jamaica, has martial law been carried into execution under circumstances of the most painful character. A man must be dead to all sentiments of humanity—must have banished mercy from the catalogue of human virtues—who can read the history of the Irish rebellion at the close of the last century,* the history of the slave insurrection in Demerara in 1823, and of the punishments then inflicted under martial law, as detailed in Mr. Martin's history of the colonies, under the head of British Guiana, or the account of the executions and scourgings after the recent outbreak in Jamaica, as shown by the report of the Royal Commissioners, without shuddering to think what human nature is capable of, when, stimulated by the fierce passions engendered by recent conflict, or by the sense of present, or recollection of past, fear, vengeance is let loose in the shape of martial law, to be exercised by a dominant class on an inferior and despised race. When it is borne in mind that, although the late insurrection in Jamaica was put down in a day, and that no resistance of any sort or kind was offered to the handful of soldiers whose presence sufficed to extinguish it, upwards of 1,000 persons suffered either death or torture, it seems time that, if martial law is to be exercised at all, it should be placed under strict and well-defined restraints, and that it should be limited to the time of actual rebellion or of armed resistance to authority. I am quite ready to admit that, if martial law can lawfully be put in force at all, the circumstances attending the recent outbreak were such as, at the first onset, to warrant its application. And even though the insurrection was at once put down, it might be well to have the means of summary and immediate punishment at hand, hanging, as it were, over the heads of the population, to strike terror into their minds in the event of any further disposition to disorder manifesting itself. But nothing of the sort did manifest itself. The mere presence of a handful of soldiers sufficed to put an end to what appeared at the outset likely to prove a formidable insurrection, but which in the result turned out to be of a totally different character. Nevertheless, martial law continued to be put in force. It appears from the report of the Royal Commissioners that 439 persons were put to death; 354 by sentence of courts-martial, 85 (most of them wantonly and

* See the 38th chapter of Mr. Massey's "History of the Reign of George IV.," vol. 4, p. 277—407, in which the details are fully gone into.

unnecessarily) in the pursuit. Six hundred persons were flogged, some under circumstances of, the most revolting cruelty, many of them women. Some of the scourges used were produced before the Commissioners, who observe that "it was painful to think that any man should have used such an instrument for the torturing of his fellow-creatures." Practically the rebellion was over within 24 hours after martial law was proclaimed, and from Colonel Nelson's despatch of the 21st October—wherein he says that, the next day after Mr. Gordon's trial being Sunday, and "there existing no military reason why the sentence should not be deferred," he had delayed its execution till the Monday—it appears that all apprehension of further disturbance in the district in which the insurrection first broke out was at an end by the 21st, the date of Mr. Gordon's trial. Fears were, no doubt, entertained of outbreaks in other parts of the island, and communications to that effect were made to the Governor by the Custodes of different parishes. But those fears proved unfounded; no further insurrection, no further disturbance took place; there was no rebellion going on for the suppression of which martial law was necessary, yet martial law went on in its sanguinary work. "On the 30th of October," say the Commissioners, "it was formally stated by the Governor 'that the wicked rebellion lately existing in certain parts of the county of Surrey had been subdued, and that the chief instigators thereof and actors therein had been visited with the punishment due to their heinous offences, and that he was certified that the inhabitants of the districts lately in rebellion were desirous to return to their allegiance.' From this day, at any rate, there could have been no necessity for that promptitude in the execution of the law which almost precluded a calm inquiry into each man's guilt or innocence. Directions might and ought to have been given that courts-martial should discontinue their sittings, and the prisoners in custody should then have been handed over for trial by the ordinary tribunals." The Commissioners, in conclusion, report that "By the continuance of martial law in its full force to the extreme limit of its statutory operation the people were deprived for a longer time than the necessary period of the great constitutional privileges by which the security of life and property is provided for. That the punishments inflicted were excessive. That the punishment of death was unnecessarily frequent. That the floggings were reckless, and at Bath positively barbarous. That the burning of 1,000 houses was wanton and cruel."

Assuming the legality of what was thus done under martial law—as to which I purposely abstain from expressing any opinion, lest any further judicial proceedings should take place —reserving to myself in such an event the exercise of a free and unfettered judgment on future discussion—I advert to the events in Jamaica only as showing the necessity for legislation if martial law is ever again to be put in force. Assuming, in like manner, that credit is to be given to the Governor and the military authorities for perfect integrity of purpose in declaring and continuing martial law, and for having been actuated in so doing by no other motive than an honest desire to do what was best for the safety of the Island, it seems to me that, the more the honesty of their conduct is insisted on, the more important it becomes to place restraints on the exercise of so despotic and dangerous a power, lest sudden panic, or undue fear, or unreflecting zeal should again lead to its immoderate use, and to the unnecessary sacrifice of human life, or infliction of human suffering. And the fact that among the educated classes of this highly-civilised community persons can be found to uphold and applaud such proceedings—though I believe very few persons who do so have taken the trouble to read the report of the Commissioners, or the evidence taken by them, or to make themselves acquainted with the facts—seems to me to render the necessity for legislation to prevent such barbarities in future only the more apparent. But of still greater importance is it that, if martial law is to be put in force, rules should be fixed for the procedure to be followed on trials under it. Above all, that where a case turns upon circumstantial evidence, time and opportunity shall be afforded to the accused to meet the charge. English legislation, looking, no doubt, to the disadvantage a man labours under who has the power of Government to contend with, and to the danger of angry passions and hostile prejudices interfering with the calm administration of justice on trials for treason, has provided additional safeguards for the protection of the accused. The prisoner, in addition to the right to have copies of the depositions as on ordinary trials, has by statute (7 Anne, c. 11, s. 21) the right to have a copy of the indictment delivered to him a fortnight before the trial, together with a list of the witnesses to be produced against him, as well as a list of the jury. On opening the *Times* of May 1st my eye alighted on the following passage from a report of the proceedings against the Fenian prisoners at Dublin :—

"Mr. Justice Fitzgerald sat half-an-hour before the usual time yesterday morning in order to assign counsel to prisoners against whom true bills had been found for high treason. When they were placed at the bar, his Lordship informed them that the grand jury had found bills of indictment against them for high treason. They were entitled to copies of the indictment, which would be furnished them either to-day or to-morrow, as also lists of the jurors and witnesses. They would be called upon to plead to the indictment found against them on Monday, the 13th of May. He had further to tell them that they were entitled to name two counsel and an attorney to act for them. If they were not prepared to do that then, they could name the professional gentlemen they wished to represent them at any time between that and the 13th of May to the governor of the prison, who would communicate their wishes to the Crown Solicitor."

Contrast this with the proceedings in Mr. Gordon's case. Taken from a place where he would have had the advantage of a regular trial, a previous knowledge of the case he had to meet, the means of defence, the presence of friends, the assistance of counsel, the cross-examination of the witnesses, the full opportunity to rebut their testimony by counter evidence, the direction to the jury of a professional and responsible judge, he is hurried off without an opportunity of communicating with any one, and transported to another part of the island, where he had neither friend nor adviser. Even a letter written to him by a friend, suggesting the line of defence, is purposely kept from him. Alone and helpless, he is immediately and with unseemly and deplorable haste put upon his trial, without knowledge of the charge till called upon to answer it, without knowledge of the facts intended to be proved, or of the witnesses intended to be examined, still less that the depositions of living witnesses taken behind his back would be brought forward against him. Under these most disadvantageous circumstances he is put upon his trial, before a court in all probability sharing in the common prepossession against him, and is condemned on evidence, in my judgment, wholly insufficient to warrant his condemnation. It may be said, it is true, that Gordon did not apply for a postponement of the trial. But of what advantage would a postponement have been to him while in total ignorance of what he had to meet? Besides which, this unhappy man appears, if one may judge from the utter want of vigour and intelligence displayed in his defence, to have been paralysed by the circumstances in which he was placed, and to have been rendered incapable of grappling with the difficulties by which he was surrounded. No one, I think, who has the faintest idea of what the administration of justice involves could deem the proceedings on this trial consistent with justice, or, to use a homely phrase, with that fair play which is the right of the commonest criminal. All I can say is, that if, on martial law being proclaimed, a man can lawfully be thus tried, condemned, and sacrificed, such a state of things is a scandal and a reproach to the institutions of this great and free country; and as a minister of justice, profoundly imbued with a sense of what is due to the first and greatest of earthly obligations, I enter my solemn and emphatic protest against the lives of men being thus dealt with in the time to come.—A. E. C.

G. NORMAN, PRINTER, MAIDEN-LANE, COVENT-GARDEN.